GW00750818

Living in Sri Lanka

james fennell & turtle bunbury

Living in Sri Lanka

with 250 color illustrations

Thames & Hudson

This book is dedicated to Joanna Connolly whose assistance in coordination and styling was so invaluable that she has since become Joanna Fennell.

First published in 2006 in hardcover in the
United States of America by
Thames & Hudson Inc., 500 Fifth Avenue,
New York, New York 10110

thamesandhudsonusa.com

Library of Congress Catalog Card Number 2005906272

ISBN-13: 978-0-500-51287-6
ISBN-10: 0-500-51287-6

Printed and bound in Singapore by CS Graphics

contents

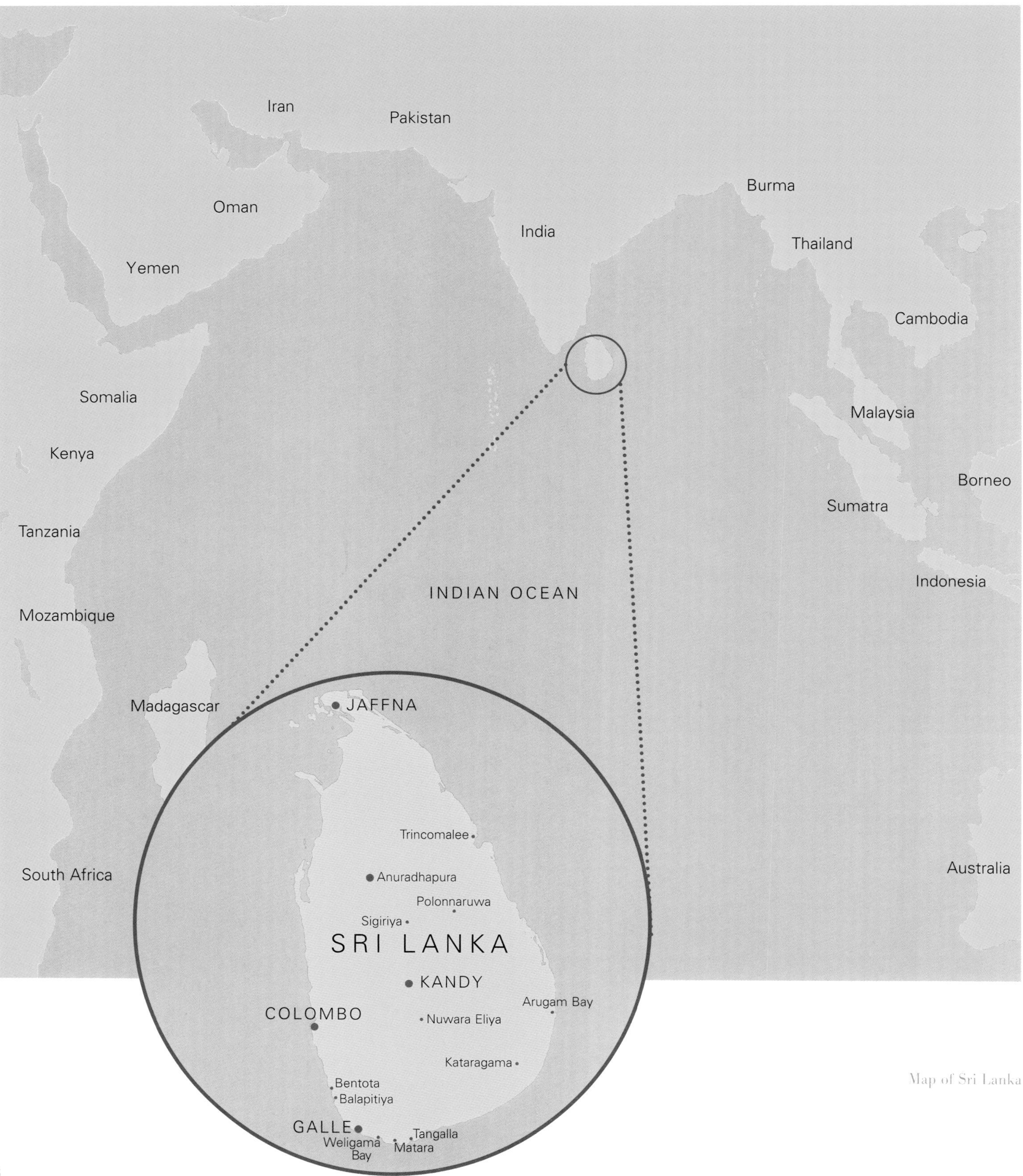

Map of Sri Lanka

introduction

The medieval Arab traders called it Serendib, the magical island of gems that once lured King Solomon to its shores. Our grandparents knew it as Ceylon, the British colony famous for tea and cricket. Since 1972 it has been Sri Lanka. Whatever its name, this tropical island off the south-western heel of India has always fired the world's imagination as a land of enchantment and beauty. Despite the damage caused by the Tsunami of Christmas 2004, Sri Lanka has and will continue to assert itself as one of the most spectacular visitor destinations on our planet. The island is simply too enigmatic for any world traveller to ignore. Almost everything about it instils the promise of paradise.

The houses, villas and hotels featured in this book reflect this new spirit of optimism. They are all unique creations, some three centuries old, others extraordinarily new. Yet they have been constructed with the utmost respect for the environment and are infused with the style and panache of their owners. The Sri Lankan people are friendly and hard-working. It's a contagious attitude that quickly transmits to anyone who visits. For the escalating number of foreigners who have decided to lay down roots on the island, the result is indeed serendipitous. Sri Lankan style has emerged, both architecturally and decoratively, into a captivating hybrid of cheerful elegance and common sense.

It is a relatively small island, about the size of Ireland, Tasmania or West Virginia. But its diversity is astounding. A thousand miles of coastline encompasses an endless curl of coconut-fringed beaches, plummeting cliffs and sumptuous bays. As one ventures inland, so the landscape starts to elevate and blossom, alluvial plains giving way to fertile plantations of exotic fruits, rubber trees and rice paddies. It is as if everything is designed to converge in the gorgeous Hill Country that runs down the centre of the island, towering over rolling jungle and lush tea plantations. The highlands mark the source of Sri Lanka's sacred rivers – the Mahawelli, the Kumbukkan Oya, the Kelani and the Manik Ganga. Elephants, monkeys and wild birds inhabit over one hundred national parks and nature reserves across the island. Such natural beauty is complemented by a unique tropical climate. Sri Lanka experiences not one, but two distinctive monsoon seasons. The happy result is that it is always perfect weather somewhere on the island. If the humidity proves unbearable or the rainfall too tedious, one simply heads for the opposite coast.

Sri Lanka is blessed with a rich culture that embraces the multi-layered influences of its Buddhist, Hindu, Muslim and Christian inhabitants. From the 3rd century BC to the 11th century AD, the island was dominated by the Sinhalese kingdom of Anuradhapura, a Buddhist-led monarchy that spearheaded the spread of enlightened Buddhist thought as far east as Thailand and Myanmar (Burma). Buddhism remains an integral part of the Sinhalese identity today, despite challenges from the Hindus of Southern India and the Tamil dominated provinces in the north of the island. In the 11th century, persistent invasions by Hindu forces from southern India compelled the king to relocate the capital to Polonnaruwa. However, by the 13th century, internal warfare ushered in an age of darkness in Sri Lankan history and both Anuradhapura and Polonnaruwa were abandoned. Rediscovered by British explorers in the 19th century, the

two ruined cities are now listed as UNESCO World Heritage Sites. Indeed Sri Lanka has seven such sites, the others being the Golden Temple of Dambulla, the city of Kandy, the Sinharaja Forest Reserve, the 1,500-year-old mountain fortress of Sigiriya and the 17th-century Dutch fort at Galle.

In the 16th century, the Catholic armies of Portugal found it remarkably easy to subjugate both the Tamil kingdom of Jaffna in the north and the Sinhalese kingdom of Kotte in the south. The mercantile forces of Dutch Puritanism superseded the Portuguese in the mid-17th century, but it was not until 1815 that British Redcoats, riding high from their victory over the French at Waterloo, were able to conquer the kingdom of Kandy in the central highlands. The complete conquest of the island initiated over a hundred years of British rule, an era notable for sweeping developments in agriculture, infrastructure and economic prosperity.

In 1948, nearly 450 years of colonial administration came to an end when Sri Lanka, or Ceylon as it was then still known, became an independent member of the British Commonwealth. There were inevitable troubles in the decades that followed as Tamils and Sinhalese struggled to establish their own sovereign rights. But the Sri Lankan people were not prepared to let factional differences destroy their homeland. The same defiant spirit commanded the national psyche in the wake of the tsunami. The moment the tidal waters began to recede, the Sri Lankan people – Tamil and Sinhalese alike – began to rebuild their coastline. Sri Lankans know that their island is a gem that dazzles every passer-by so that now more than ever before, tourism is a vital mainstay of the economy.

Defining Sri Lankan style is a necessarily complex process. The country's history, location and multi-ethnic population has left it open to influences from across the world. The possibilities offered by the current age of travel can only enhance the varied and diverse nature of global design. And yet, in terms of both architecture and style, Sri Lanka still possesses a unique and enchanting character.

Sri Lanka's vibrant history is, of course, one of the overriding influences on its architectural heritage. One need only visit the ruined cities of Anuradhapura, Polonnaruwa or Sigiriya to see the brilliance of the ancient stonemasons. The arrival of the Europeans brought new innovations. Under the Portuguese, the traditional open-air courtyards were complemented by covered verandahs and high-pitched terracotta roofs. With colonies as far apart as South Africa and Indonesia, the Dutch developed the technique still further, most notably in Galle Fort, incorporating new and often ingenious concepts of sanitation and ventilation. Six of the Galle villas, all restored in the past decade, are to found in this book. The British, buoyed by the industrial revolution in Europe, continued the tradition and brought their own ecclesiastical and secular styles to the island.

The climate has also been of pivotal importance. The island's weather commands absolute respect. Natural ventilation remains essential not just for the circulation of fresh air, but also to prevent mould and bacteria infesting the structure. Hence, Sri Lankan houses are open to the elements. Colonnaded verandahs and elaborate balconies wander along brightly coloured latticed walls and cool floors of polished cement. Cobbled courtyards and tropical gardens rise through the very centre of buildings.

Water is an inherent part of modern living, a source of health and solace. Even in towns and cities, rock ponds bubble amid cobble-rimmed courtyards, rainwater trickles down metal drainage chains, power showers poke their heads from the gnarly boughs of jakfruit trees, sleek black taps deliver fresh water into huge bathtubs of polished terrazzo. Along the south-west coast, villas sprawl between wind-blown coconut groves and the Indian Ocean. North of the pilgrim city of Kataragama, a wandering gem merchant has built a hamlet of thatched huts along the banks of the Manik Ganga, the fabled River of Gems. On the west coast at Balapitiya, a restored cinnamon planter's villa rolls down to the estuarine waters of the Madhu Ganga. In the jungles east of Colombo, tree houses overlook the mighty Kelani. North again at Ulpotha, a two-thousand-year-old reservoir provides the backdrop for a sumptuous 21st-century eco-village. Where water flows, abundance often verges on unruliness. In the highlands, the branches of the jungle require regular appointments with the garden shears as they persistently clamber over balconies and snake across the rooftops.

Sri Lanka's impoverished status in the latter decades of the 20th century left some of its older buildings in a poor and paltry state. However, in the past decade, many of these structures have been restored, both by Sri Lankan and foreign owners. Their fundamental charm has been retained and indeed often enhanced by the addition of new features, from polished cement floors and staircases to custom-built furniture and colourful fabrics. It goes without saying that the trend for restoring more of Sri Lanka's architectural treasures will be high on the agenda as the country increases its hold on the imagination of global tourism.

Aside from restorations, a number of new additions have sprung up since the late 1990s, most notably along the "Serendib Riviera" of the south-west coast. Some of Asia's most exciting architects have been employed in these projects, most notably Sri Lanka's Geoffrey Bawa. Mahawella, Bawa's last private house, indicates a man still very much on the crest of his genius on the eve of his death in 2002. Regarded as Bawa's spiritual heir, Channa Daswatta's work has received global acclaim, and a new spa complex (the Lighthouse Hotel) reflects his continued authority on the architectural landscape. Bruce Fell-Smith's hand is in evidence at the new villa, Kahanda Kanda, outside Galle, while Sonny Chan's Apa Villa is also suggestive of an architect from whom much is yet to come.

In conjunction with the architectural boom, a new wave of interior designers, furniture-makers and artists has arisen in Sri Lanka. Colombo's boutique shops brought the island's remarkable talent for handicrafts and fabrics to the fore. Behind the scenes, designers such as Niki Harrison, Shanth Fernando and Nayantara Fonseka are making their mark on the future of Sri Lankan style. Artists such as Saskia Pringers and Nuria Lamsdorff and craftsmen like Lucina Talib and the Bentota Workshop are likewise illustrative of an exciting new dawn for Sri Lankan art and design.

Sri Lanka's rich history and excellent climate combine with bold confidence and a discerning aestheticism to create an unforgettable architectural landscape. This is an island that stands proud of the past, prepared for the future but, right now, content to sit back and enjoy the glory of the present.

FATIMA
SHRINE

79 leyn baan street ▪ lighthouse street ▪ the dome ▪ galle face court
parrawa street ▪ colombo house ▪ 33rd lane ▪ middle street
doornberg ▪ 10 leyn baan street

▪ town & city

Colombo is an exciting, lively, noisy, vibrant, chaotic swirl of a city. Cranes swing from every horizon, erecting the high-rise apartment and office blocks that spell a new and prosperous debut for the island's most populated city. The ancient seafarers of Cathay, Persia and Morocco knew of Colombo, but it was not truly developed as a port until the arrival of the Portuguese in the 16th century. However, Colombo's vulnerability to the monsoons gave the Port of Galle a superior advantage until 1874 when the British Government erected a breakwater, paving the way for Colombo's evolution as the capital city.

As the 21st century progresses, so Sri Lanka's intrinsic understanding of its unique multi-cultural style has begun to force its way onto the city's main shopping streets. A series of top quality interior design stores, such as Paradise Road and Barefoot, run alongside superior fashion boutiques like Odel's and Serendib. New café bars, restaurants and art galleries are also springing up regularly as further evidence of the city's growing cosmopolitan confidence. And alongside these streets stand the Buddhist and Hindu temples of the 18th century, the British colonial banks and offices of the 19th and the twin towers of the World Trade Centre, 34 stories high and faced in reflecting glass. Visitors to Sri Lanka can hardly avoid staying a night or two in Colombo but, though it may be a large and boisterous city, it is determined to give the visitor a good reason to stay. Amongst the many businesses to relocate from Galle to Colombo after 1874 was Macan Markar Gems, the company who built Galle Face Courts One and Two on the city's waterfront. Two former storage depots (see Galle Face Court, The Dome) in the Macan Markar towers have lately been converted into stunning residential apartments. In the suburbs, three distinct 19th century townhouses have been converted and renovated to suit the requirements of the modern age.

A frenetic highway runs parallel to the ocean along the west coast of the island between Colombo and Galle. The latter port was established by the Portuguese in 1505 after one of their fleets, sailing around India, was driven to shelter by a storm and obliged to drop anchor. The port flourished as Sri Lanka's principal maritime trade base until eclipsed by Colombo in the 1870s. Galle continued to prosper under the Dutch, who walled the Fort, and the British. During the 19th century, an increasing number of Muslim traders settled in the merchant villas, enhancing the Fort's inimitable blend of European style and Asian tradition. Classified as a UNESCO World Heritage Site in 1988, the Fort and surrounding town are today awash with colour and vitality. Many of the original Dutch villas have been restored in recent years by a wave of personable characters, some Sri Lankan, others international. Five such villas feature in the following pages, each one a unique distillation of the original structure and the personal desires and styles of its current occupants. Overlooking the Fort from a nearby rise is 300-year-old Doornberg, the magnificently restored former residence of the Dutch commander.

79 leyn baan street

Leyn Baan Street takes its name from the Dutch word for "rope walk" recalling a time when, under Dutch control, the street was populated by merchants involved in the manufacture of coir-rope for fishing vessels. During the 19th century, the north east quarter of Galle Fort became the demesne of a hard-working, largely Muslim community. They gradually acquired the villas of the disbanded Dutch VOC merchants and converted them in their own fashion.

Born in South Wales, Olivia Richli had been working for Adrian Zecha's Aman Resorts in Java for the best part of a decade when, in the summer of 1998, she made her debut trek to Sri Lanka. President Soeharto of Indonesia had just fallen from power and her future in the archipelago looked precarious. On arriving in Sri Lanka, she instantly made her way to Taprobane Island for a week. She then called in at the New Oriental Hotel in Galle Fort, a colonial hotel established in 1863. The New Oriental Hotel was in serious disarray but the fundamental charm of its past wooed Olivia almost as much as its captivating owner, Nesta Brohier, a third generation hotelier. Zecha and Brohier were friends. Richli suspected that any day now, Zecha would take a keen interest in the New Oriental Hotel.

Within a few days, Richli was sketching a map of Galle Fort, mastering its grid-work of streets and squares. On her next visit, she befriended the Edens and secured the assistance of the inimitable Charlie Hulse. Hulse escorted her on a tour of Fort villas then up for sale. It was the sixth one, located in the Islamic quarter, which stopped Richli in her tracks. "The minute I walked in the front door I knew this was the house I wanted." The villa was built for a Dutch merchant in about 1780. After the flight of the Dutch in the early 19th century, it was acquired by a series of Moorish families. The owner, Mrs Thaha, an elderly Muslim widow, was keen to settle somewhere more suited to her advanced age.

"Our family had been wanderers for a long time," says Richli. "I wanted something more permanent. I'd never heard of Galle before I came to Sri Lanka. Now it has become one of the most important parts of my life."

Assisted by Hulse, Richli set about "rejigging" the property. "I was charmed the instant I saw it so I really didn't want to change much." A dilapidated garage was dismantled and converted into garden. A stone wall was erected to the rear of the property on what had previously consisted of

above A wrought iron bed stands modestly on flagstones, animated by an orange and red bedspread from Jodhpur, Rajasthan, and by the soft ochre hue of the wall.
opposite Like many of Galle Fort's 18th century villas, a bright, open-air courtyard occupies the very centre of the building. Colonnaded flagstone walkways flank a rectangular pond featuring two granite water-troughs from Borobudur in Java. A rustic double door to the right leads into the kitchen while the balcony above the main entrance is bathed in morning light. The walls are painted with *samirah*, a local ochre mixed with limewash. This traditional Sri Lankan finish requires annual maintenance but the limewash does much to keep insects at bay. The hanging chains are a traditional alternative to drainpipes; rainwater gushes directly down into the pond during monsoon downpours.

below Sri Lanka has witnessed the remarkable success of the application of cement to modern design, as seen in the splendid concrete dining table featured here. The owner also added the concrete and wood verandah in place of the original covered terrace. A Jatilan horse, used in Javanese trance dances, stands atop a glass front cabinet, also from Java.

opposite left "Kursi Cowboy" or cowboy chairs from Java surround a thick slab of teak surmounted on two timber trunks to make a table. Through the arches to the rear, the courtyard runs into the outer yard.

opposite right The kitchen exudes a simple, homely ambience from its terracotta floor to the cream and vanilla coloured shelves of concrete and wood.

odious open-drains, smoldering rubbish heaps and a corrugated shack. Storage rooms were turned into bathrooms, windows were refitted and the doors stripped back to their original colour. Other than that, the layout remains effectively the same, right down to the cooker installed where Mrs Thala's open fire formerly stood.

The junk-covered rooftop was simultaneously transformed into an open sitting area beholding Galle's lighthouse, the Indian Ocean and the rising headland of Rhumasala in the distance. According to the epic Hindu legends of the *Ramyana*, Rhumasala was created from herbs accidentally dropped by Hanuma while returning from the Himalayas to help her wounded lover, Lakshmana. The headland certainly boasts an extraordinary eco-system, and is home to trees, plants and herbs found nowhere else in Sri Lanka. The crackled granite rock also registers the third highest incidence of lightning in the world.

Six times a day, the peace of Galle Fort is broken by the sound of the *muzzein*, the Muslim's call to prayer. But when Olivia tells how the *muzzein* is in fact a live cantation by an amusing old man named Aun, the sense of intimacy is restored. In 1998, the Aman Resorts acquired the New Oriental Hotel. In November 2003, Richli was appointed to oversee the renovation. The hotel reopened in December 2004 under the new name of Amangella. In the meantime, Richli strolls the streets, acknowledging greetings, fending off job-seekers and politely refusing strange women who say "hallo, you like to buy a house?"

opposite On the upper balcony red and pink bougainvillea surround a sofa on the outer patio. In the background, Galle's landmark lighthouse rises into the sky, while the Fort's 450-year-old walls run to its north.
right Upstairs, the walls of the master bedroom are a soothing shade of blue, made from a mixture of limewash and Rinso washing powder. A custom-made mosquito net from Bali hangs over the bed. Pillows from Tuban, East Java, are made of indigo batik on hand-woven cotton. On the right, two sets of blue double doors lead out to the flower-filled balcony overlooking the inner courtyard. All the rooms in this villa seem to have numerous different doorways leading from them, perhaps as part of the original air circulation system. A simple Sri Lankan rug of woven bamboo lies upon the wooden plank floor.

lighthouse street

"I have come to corrupt the foreigners," says Rohan Jayakody with a mischievous smile, referring to his 2003 acquisition of No. 50 Lighthouse Street in Galle Fort. The enigmatic Sri Lankan florist has been making gentle waves in his homeland ever since his return from London in the early 1980s. Jayakody's Sri Lankan properties include a Geoffrey Bawa house in Colombo, a Victorian plantation villa in the Hill Country and the Gunasekera House in Bentota. But his villa in Galle ranks as his favourite by a considerable distance. "It's like a Vermeer painting, only more vulgar," he suggests. (A neighbour feels Caravaggio is more apt. It is certainly decadent and, by Sri Lankan standards, outrageous.)

Few who pass by its discreet wooden doors would guess what lies beyond. Perhaps they might take a second glance at the imperial vases standing sentry on the steps. Or maybe catch a fleeting reflection in the curved mirror surmounting the fretwork above the door. And conceivably there are scholars amongst them who could translate the French motto overhead. (*Honi soit qui mal et pense!*)

On entering the property, one is instantly dazzled by a sensual kaleidoscope of animal heads, massive wooden sculptures, leafy foliage, dangling chandeliers and gigantic urns running perhaps 200 metres towards a stone wall lit by blossoming sunshine. The ground floor is essentially a single flagstone corridor, no more than eight metres wide, rising up an occasional step. Walls on either side of the corridor, retaining the roughness of their 250-year-old past, are painted a faded orange. All doors and columns were salvaged from an early 18th century Portuguese manor house in the fishing village of Mirissa.

The entrance hall is dominated by more than eighty pair of antlers, mounted on handcrafted wooden deer heads, some of an extremely unlikely disposition, others convincing. Complimented by three massive tea chests, the hall creates an illusion of a quintessentially colonial home. However, one's eye is soon drawn to a veritable cabinet of curiosities, fronted by a collection of enormous processional sculptures from Jaffna – flying horses, a demonic tiger, an astonished Mary Magdalene, a pot-bellied magician. As if to magnify the absurdity of this group, a giant copper telescope stands to the left, pointed through leafy bamboo towards the open skies. The effect is something akin to a Moroccan souk. "It is an absolute folly," says the owner happily.

Perhaps to temper this sudden onslaught of decadence, the first seating area is more restrained. Two five-seater sofas

above Imperial vases flank the double doors through which the villa is accessed from Lighthouse Street. Above the door, a bas-relief is engraved with *Honi Soit Qui Mal et Pense* (Shame on him who thinks this evil). The Portuguese inspired doors and columns were acquired from an early 18th physician's house in Mirissa.

opposite Looking back towards the main entrance, the horseshoe arches and rough flagstone floor recalls the villa's Moorish essence. Mounted on a cement cube to the left, a wooden statue of a Mary Magdalene beckons.

Mobilgas
Mobilgas

face each other, separated by a low wooden table. On the walls, portraits of Jayakody's forebears stare bemusedly at a pair of oriental scrolls depicting a high ranking Chinese official and his wife. The assemblage of portraits briefly reasserts the colonial theme but the villa swiftly returns to the bazaar style when a guest's bedroom, concealed by a grill, drops unexpectedly into the room, drawing one still deeper into the building.

The next "carriage", with its low blue ceiling, contains the kitchen, granted centre stage, the sinks and cooker hidden behind a lattice screen. An ochre archway then merges into a small dining area, furnished with planters' chairs and an antique wardrobe, before culminating in an elevated open-air space of giant oil vases, cement blocks, a coconut tree and a shower, stunningly enclosed in a wall of coral rock. The outdoor garden area enhances the extravagant flavour of a Roman atrium villa.

The ground floor corridor is essentially Jayakody's reception room. The real high jinks go on upstairs, either in the lacquered black bar on the first floor, or on a flamboyant rooftop of moulded cement sofas, scattered peacock feathers and bamboo-roofed shelters. From here one has an exceptional view of the surrounding landscape, a sea of terracotta rooftops and frothy green treetops, broken intermittently by the ocean, the white towers of the Dutch Kirk and the Lighthouse itself.

Shortly before our arrival, Jayakody hosted a dinner party where, in traditional Sri Lankan style, the guests drank, danced, ate and departed in that order. One wonders how his neighbours – one Islamic, the other Hindu – reacted to the sounds of Indian rap music echoing down the street. The important thing is that Jayakody is Sri Lankan and proud of it. His focus is on the future and he is determined life should be lived with as much enjoyment as possible. As the inscription above his door reads: "Shame on him who thinks this evil!"

far left The flagstone corridor is dominated by ornately decorated processional sculptures from Jaffna. The 18th century collection includes two "Flying Pegasus" horses in rearing position, a demonic tiger and Suran, a bare bellied gentleman with big ears and a moustache. To the rear is a giant copper telescope by Cooke & Sons of Yorkshire.

left Some eighty pairs of deer antlers are mounted on wooden heads on the wall above the inner entrance door. Each pair was individually carved in the 19th century for various British manor houses along the south coast. A pair of beautifully lacquered Chinese spice urns from Indonesia stand either side of the arch.

below Looking through the building towards the kitchen, the right side of the first seating area is hung with two charismatic scroll portraits of a red-robed Chinese official and his wife. A 17th century brass chandelier hangs over a low wooden table simply decorated with bowls and bells.

below A wooden staircase rises above the kitchen to the guest's bedroom on the mezzanine floor. Meals are taken on the oval table to the centre of the room. Crockery and cutlery are kept in the wardrobe on the right. Above the wardrobe stands a marble bust of Thomas Jefferson.

opposite top left Lower level seating options on the rooftop behold a sea of terracotta red roofs and verdant green treetops. A simple coconut fibre mattress and large silk coated oval pillow lie upon an elevated polished concrete bed. The blue tiles were rescued from a demolished 19th century British tea bungalow.

opposite top right The rooftop has been sensitively converted into an outdoor living room, particularly popular during the owner's sporadic parties. A bamboo roof laden with coloured glass-lamps hangs from four samara columns. Polished concrete benches form a U-shape around a black and yellow tiled floor. Black timber railings add to the sense of security.

above left The master bedroom opens out onto a mezzanine floor, tiled yellow and black, and culminating with a black timber staircase. An old wooden park bench sits nonchalantly against the left wall.

above right Looking from the kitchen through to the rear garden. In the foreground stands a round table and two chairs. A pair of planters' chairs rest beneath the ochre coloured arch. The wall to the rear was made of pale coral rock from the south west coast; the black lattice timber door conceals an outdoor shower. Giant oil vases and antique furniture enhance the impression of a Roman atrium villa.

the dome

The Galle Face Court in Colombo was built in 1923 by Sir Muhammad Macan Markar, a prominent Muslim politician and gem merchant who once owned the largest star sapphire in the world. The 182-carat gem, discovered in Sri Lanka in 1907, was subsequently bequeathed to the Smithsonian Institute by Mary Pickford and is now, misleadingly, called the "Star of Bombay". The Galle Face Court, built upon old British army horse stables, was part of his dream. Fireworks exploded across the seafront when the six-storey apartment block opened.

After Sri Lanka gained independence in 1948, the Galle Face Court went into predictable decline. The original tenants, commercial employees and civil servants, moved out. Chaotic jungles of electrical wire began creeping down the high ceilings. Hairline cracks erupted along the wide, sweeping corridors. Sir Muhammed's grandson, Hamza Macan Markar, was eager to halt the rot. During the 1990s, a new wave of foreign businessmen began to settle in Colombo. The American jewelry designer Dick Dumas moved into one of the apartments. Francis Leighton, one of Sri Lanka's great "Social Butterflies" took on another.

In 2001, Mr Macan Markar was approached by Giles Scott, co-founder of the Ulpotha eco-retreat north of Kandy (see page 158). Scott expressed a desire to take on the uppermost floor of the Court. Mr Macan Markar was mildly confused. The top floor consisted of a single dome-roofed room, used as a storage depot for half a century's worth of discarded relics. There were, however, some elders who remembered watching the sun set on the Ocean back when the floor below was used as a badminton court.

Scott has since converted the floor into one of the most remarkable apartments in Colombo. It was a relatively straightforward project. The room was emptied of all junk. The walls were repainted, first an off-white and lately with special luminous paint that comes to life when ultra-violet lights come on. White cement was carefully poured upon the floor and polished to a smooth, clear finish. Useful alcoves were carved into the thick pillars separating the windows. A roof terrace submerged in electrical wires, television aerials and telephone cables was converted into the master bedroom with its own balcony facing over the Galle Face Hotel towards the Indian Ocean.

The Dome's role as an "observatory" seems to be confirmed by the eighteen windows which now form one of the principal features of the apartment. These elegant wooden-framed windows are set into the curved wall in

above Dusk settles on the Galle Face Court, the purple lights of the Dome illuminating the twilight. This highly desirable city apartment was formerly used as a storage space for the luggage of colonial civil servants working in the area.

opposite and overleaf As the sun sinks into the horizon of the Indian Ocean, the changing spectrum of the interior lights becomes an extension of the reddening dusk. The lighting options in the dome are numerous and diverse, adjustable to suit the mood of the owner. The spectrum ranges from a dense blue haze created by sixteen fluorescent tube lights, inspired by the American artist, James Turrell, to an ultraviolet deep seascape depicting an enormous whale shark and school of jellyfish.

groups of three. Each window frames an alternative view of the Colombo skyline; kites flying on Galle Face Green, the wind-ruffled waters of Beira Lake, the promenade stretching towards the Indian Ocean. "At this height, the air is much fresher than at street level," explains Scott. "Mastering the ventilation system was a process of elimination. As the seasons change, I've learned that if you open two or three different windows then the air channels change. So if you get it right, there's no need for fans or air-conditioning, no matter how humid it is outside."

The domed ceiling is also an immense feature. Scott sagely treats it as a vast canvas on which he can continually experiment with innovative designs. Assisted by artists from Sri Lanka and abroad, past incarnations have included an earthy green globe, an Arabian howdah and a minimalist blue backdrop supporting an illuminated polystyrene ball. The brilliant underwater scene pictured here was painted by the Spanish artist, Nuria Lamsdorff.

below The master bedroom features a side table set on a concrete cube, a red oriental cabinet and bamboo ladder from Java, serving as a towel rack
opposite left The bedroom's private balcony beholds the sun setting over the ocean.

galle face court

With a population bordering on three million, Colombo is not a city preparing to sleep. Far from it, the Sri Lankan capital is ablaze with energy, stimulated by foreign investment from China and Europe, encapsulated in a horizon of cranes erecting new buildings as far as the eye can see. But for foreigners living in Sri Lanka, it is sometimes important to have a base in the capital from which to arrange one's affairs and perhaps take advantage of the impressive array of boutiques.

Since moving to Sri Lanka, Jack and Jo Eden have been regular voyagers along the frenetic highway that runs down the west coast from Colombo to Galle. Head-quartered in Galle, their successful "Eden Villas" business involves the marketing of some twenty villas on the south coast to international tourists. In 1999, they acquired the lease of an apartment in the Galle Face Court, a four storey block belonging to the Macan Markar family, located next to Colombo's famous Galle Face Hotel. The ground floor apartment was in dire condition, having been used as a storage depot for scaffolding since the 1960s. The original cement floor was badly cracked and, in many areas, had completely disintegrated. Sprawling balls of unidentified electrical wires, some live, were suspended from the seven-metre ceiling. The doors were so thickly painted in overcoat they were no longer able to move. There was neither bathroom nor kitchen and a courtyard to the rear had become a rubbish dump for the entire building.

Over the next four years, the Edens gradually cleared out the apartment and restored it to its original condition. They then improved upon this by the addition of a kitchen and bathroom on the right side of the main living area. A double door now leads directly from the lobby into the apartment's main living room, an expansive area of high ceilings and thick stone walls, flooded with light from a series of big french windows. A floor of polished cement and parquet runs the course of the apartment, before merging into an intimate, freshly planted walled garden. To the right of the living room lies the kitchen, and three bedrooms, each room benefiting from an inspired coat of paint and polished white floors.

above Looking from the rear wall of the garden back towards the wooden doors of the living room. The garden was created out of a space previously used as a dumping ground. Honeysuckle now grows around the entrance.

opposite The living room floor was cleaned, scraped and polished back to its original teak colour. In the foreground, two 1940s barber chairs from Kandy face across an Indonesian table to a full-length nude commissioned by Jack Eden to celebrate his tenth wedding anniversary to wife, Jo. Beneath the painting stands a 700-year-old Tibetan chest covered in hand-painted leather, and surmounted by a pair of green lacquered Vietnamese wedding baskets. A mahogany day-bed from Hong Kong stands opposite a sofa made by Colombo's Paradise Road studio. Doors to the rear of the room open out to the garden. Above the bronze Buddha statue to the left is a watercolour by Sri Lankan artist, Anoma Wijewardene. Sesaths and other traditional good luck charms are used as decorative items. The sculpture in the far left is by local artist, Manoranjana Herath.

Raised in Hong Kong, Jo Eden has always understood that small spaces can seem much bigger if the design concept is right. Her close involvement with the new wave of exclusive villas and hotels erupting across southern Sri Lanka has clearly enhanced her own inimitable eye for the aesthetic. She has styled the living room as an elegant, yet dreamy retreat, enlivened by colourful works by upcoming Sri Lankan artists which hang upon the walls. The fabrics were sourced locally in shops such as Barefoot and Paradise Road, while Jo designed the living room sofa. Furniture is minimal, the intention being to keep this apartment-cum-office as uncluttered as possible. And yet for all that, there is something delightfully familiar about it, as if one is forever dreaming of opening the front door and saying: "Honey, I'm home".

above Looking from the entrance through to the living room. On the walls are works by local artists Jagath Ravindra (smallest) and Manoranjana Herath (on left) and Indian artist, Philomena Pawar (large blue). The lantern above the door is from an antique shop in Galle.

opposite Bedrooms are sophisticated and uncluttered with antique wardrobes set behind a four-poster bed of brass capped wrought iron. A dressing room stands to the right. All doors are original teak; some fifteen layers of paint were stripped to restore their natural colour.

parrawa street

A stone street leads directly from the Indian Ocean to Charles Hulse's house on Galle Fort's Parrawa Street. The street is bound on either side by villas, many over 250 years old, built when Dutch spice merchants were in control of the country. American-born Hulse moved to Sri Lanka in 1974, fresh from two decades on the Greek island of Hydra. He settled on the south coast some miles west of the Fort, which had by then fallen into considerable decline. In 1987 Hulse seized an opportunity and purchased a rundown villa, previously used as a brothel, on the Fort's south side. Assisted by a team of local carpenters and builders, Hulse set to work restoring the property. Plywood partitions installed in the early 20th century were replaced with three arches, opening onto a small courtyard, flanked by two adjacent wings. The terracotta roof was simultaneously raised "Arkansas-style", waterproofed and re-laid.

The property consists of a living room, dining room, library, kitchen and three bedrooms. The courtyard occupies the space between the kitchen wing and guest bedrooms to the rear of the property. Hulse installed a small pool in the yard, shaded beneath a fragrant frangipani and a guava tree. A floor of polished white cement runs throughout the property, echoing the vibrant white of the walls and sofa covers. The white not only brightens the interior but also provides an excellent backdrop for Hulse's eclectic art collection.

Hulse has enjoyed an eventful life. Raised in Arkansas during the Depression, he escaped to San Francisco at the age of fourteen and became a tap-dancer. He served with the US Airforce for three years during the Korean War, before embarking on a long Broadway run with Yul Brynner and Patricia Morrison in *The King and I*. He danced at the Lido in Paris in the 1950s before returning to San Francisco to teach dancing. He lived variously in Normandy and Hydra, before settling in Sri Lanka where he wrote the novel, *In Tall Cotton*.

When Hulse finished restoring his Galle townhouse, he invited friends to come and stay. Month after month, travellers from afar would tentatively make their way down Parrawa Street and "swing by Charlie's for a Bloody Mary". Those who got lost in the maze of the Fort's streets were wont

above The library lies through an arch to the right of the entrance. Above an 18th century English desk hangs *The Harlequin* by Italian artist, Russo. A torso sculpture from Australia stands to the left of a desk. On the table in the front right is an ornate bronze piece from a Thai palanquin, found at an archaeological dig near the ancient palace of Sigiriya. On the table in the front left are two Buddhist statuettes, acquired locally. An 18th century French Provincial sofa is bedecked with blue and white cushions, designed by Barbara Sansoni and purchased at Barefoot in Colombo.

opposite An art deco clock hangs between the two arches leading from the drawing room through to the pool. Beneath the clock, a silver jewelry cabinet surmounts a wooden tea chest. To the right of the potted plant, lies an oak and cane "traveling bed" with brass wheels and green leather cushions.

SEIKOSHA

to marvel at the number of villas scattered through the coastal citadel – 473 according to the Sri Lankan Archaeological Department. At length, Jack and Jo Eden, a British couple based in Hong Kong, took the plunge and became the second foreign owners of a Galle Fort villa. Hulse was swiftly recruited as a consultant for the restoration. With more than fifty villas now in foreign ownership, Hulse's "retirement" is regularly interrupted by the clang of his doorbell as another newcomer seeks advice on where to find a decent electrician or carpenter.

Hulse's villa is something of a shrine to his past lives. While keepsakes from his Arkansas childhood are few – "I haven't been back in a hundred years" – the walls feature works collected during his time in France and Hydra by the likes of Georgia O'Keeffe, Nissan Engel, Ena de Silva, Dimitri Gassomis and Sam Fisher. Likewise he has amassed many first-rate antique pieces on his travels – French, English, Italian, American and Sri Lankan – which now furnish his villa. But for Hulse, his preferred location is sitting by the pool, Bloody Mary in hand, perhaps discussing the pros and cons of Sri Lankan real estate with a young couple passing through.

left Close up of *Aged Greeks* by Sam Fisher and *Two Fish* by A. Fancho of St Tropez. The grey and white striped cushions are from France.

opposite The dining room lies through a double archway to the right of the pool. An early 18th century Italian Provincial table and French Provincial chairs are capable of seating twelve. Above an almirah sideboard to the rear, hangs *Red Poppy* by American artist, Georgia O'Keeffe. An elaborate plaster sculpture by French artist Roselynn Granet from the early 1980s doubles as a lampshade above the table.

left The rich blue tiles of the pool lend an enchanting sense of tropical location to the rear of the property. A guava and a frangipani, decorated in Dutch style lanterns, offer shade from the right side of the pool. A stone elephant designed by Ena de Silva appears to drink from the pool's edge.

above Simple wicker chairs, painted white, are grouped around a polished marble table on the upper verandah above the pool. The terracotta roofs of Galle Fort supply a skyline through the columns. A temple door engraved with the image of a Hindu prince hangs on the rear wall.

colombo house

In the early 20th century, the Cinnamon Gardens north of Colombo consisted of a series of small cinnamon estates set around rural gentry houses. This 1920s house was originally built for the Wijanathens, a well-to-do Sinhalese family famous for hosting musical soirees after dinner. In 2001 the present owner leased the property to Bob and Nikki Harrison. They took an apartment in the Galle Face Court while setting about the renovation. This involved installing new windows in the dining room, reshaping the drawing room, adding the white wooden lattice to the staff quarters and extending the 1930s kitchen. They erected a small *ambalama* (a traditional Sri Lankan open-air pavilion) at the rear of the house, planted a garden and laid a new driveway. A frangipani hedge runs the length of the property affording a welcome sense of privacy.

A sleek black gate off Gregory's Road leads to a driveway of beautiful riverstones, handpicked from the Mahdu Ganga. To the right, a grass lawn rolls up towards the white colonial house. A verandah runs around the front of the house, its polished cement floor painted egg-white. Teak doorways from the verandah lead into the principal drawing room. Four sofas run back to back on teakwood floorboards down the centre of the room. A large gilded mirror magnifies the size of the room, reflecting a pretty canvas of a boat adrift on a lily pond. Glass bowls on glass top tables contain candles and flower petals. To the rear of the room, two full size wooden sculptures stand sentry beside the doors leading into the dining area. Every piece has been meticulously placed to enhance the sense of space and yet the room manages to retain an ambience of informality.

Taking its cue from the colonial Dutch houses of Ceylon and South Africa, the bedrooms and library are disposed to the left and right of the drawing room. High ceilings and the exact positioning of doorways convey the original architect's skilled understanding of proportion. The library is an informal room uplifted by the light pouring in through six wooden arch-windows, each one stripped back to its natural colour. Books range from airport thrillers to the heady memoirs of 18th century French aristocrats.

The drawing room duly unfolds into the dining room and kitchen area, marking a more recent development. One of the Wijanathen family, an executive with Ceylon Railways, took a somewhat utilitarian approach in adding a curvaceous, cantilevered staircase and erecting iron girders across the lower roof. The staircase was formerly boarded up in teak panelling. The Harrisons removed the panelling and waxed the staircase to its current finish, creating the round alcoves at its base. The dining room has been carefully stylized with contemporary tables and chairs.

above This splendid Colombo townhouse was built in the 1920s by a prosperous Sri Lankan family. The exterior exudes the confidence of British Ceylon with its classical horseshoe arches and imperial balcony.

opposite Four sofas run back to back on teakwood floors down the centre of the drawing room. To the rear, two Sri Lankan temple guards stand either side of the dining room doors. On the back wall hangs a painting by Sri Lankan artist, Mahen Perera.

To the rear of the house the *ambalama* is bedecked with stone candle holders, wooden bowls of nutshells and ostrich eggs, and large urns laden with ferns. This is where the Harrisons and their guests tend to recline, submerged in newspapers and catching the last rays of sunshine before night falls.

above Above the dining room, an open air reading room enjoys a cooling breeze throughout the day. Guests recline in planter's chairs and sofas bedecked in fabrics from Paradise Road, Colombo. A coir carpet made locally traverses the floor.

right The owners have recently built an *ambalama* in the garden at the rear of the house. Polished grey cement cubes bookend a pair of bamboo chaise-longues, the table between casually decorated with ostrich eggs, stone owls and wooden bowls of forest nuts. Lattice wood-panelling in the background keeps the staff quarters airy.

A series of six arched double doors lead off the library, each supporting its own Burmese teak framed windows. A wrought iron glass-top table stands centre stage upon a zebra skin rug. Armchairs in the style of Frank Lloyd Wright and navy blue sofas made locally surround the room.

Provence Interiors

left One of the original owners worked with the Sri Lankan railway. He took a somewhat utilitarian approach to the design, adding a low-stepped kitchen staircase. The staircase has been opened up by the Harrisons and now forms one of the major features to the rear of the house. A polished concrete kitchen table, inspired by Geoffrey Bawa's own work-top, stands in front of aquamarine kitchen cupboards.

above A 1930s wing has been converted into the dining room, located at the end of the reception room. The dining room furniture was all designed by the owners and made locally.

33rd lane

Built in the 1880s, Mrs Norma Tennekoon's two-storey townhouse is situated at the end of 33rd Lane, a cul-de-sac just off Bagatelle Road in Kollupitiya, Colombo. The surrounding area was formerly part of the Bagatalle Walawa, later "Alfred House", a 120-acre farm owned by the great philanthropist Charles de Soysa. At the time the Tennekoon house was built, de Soysa owned nearly 25,000 acres of coffee, coconut and cinnamon plantations across Sri Lanka. The houses on 33rd Lane were probably built for senior workers on the Bagatelle estate.

Mrs Tennekoon purchased the property in 1976 on the advice of her friend, Geoffrey Bawa, the architect who had rented a series of bungalows on 33rd Lane as his home and studio since 1959. Bawa was rarely able to suppress his passion for the private house, especially for those who lived within range of his vision. And so he swiftly commenced a renovation to make the house more suitable to the widowed Mrs Tennekoon's lifestyle. Her late husband, Herbert Tennekoon, was onetime Secretary to the Treasury and, after retirement, served as Sri Lanka's Ambassador to Japan. Bawa began to rearrange the building, raising roofs, knocking down walls, inserting a verandah and creating a new L-shaped living room. By 1978 Mrs Tennekoon's house was amongst the most admired in Colombo.

A small door on the right side of 33rd Lane leads into a small, elegant courtyard, cobbled with stones from the old Fort – Pettah tramline. Brass lamps and Cambodian dragons flank a sofa of tamarind wood. A small sculpture of the Hindu God Ganesh stands upon a series of stacked copper pots, deliberately left unpolished. The principal rooms lie through a set of double doors at the far side of the courtyard. It is effectively a sequence of rooms, connected by open arches, culminating with an Italianate garden of leafy ferns, curvaceous bamboos, hanging baskets and a raised terracotta pond.

In the main living room, a floor of cobble-fringed cement flagstones is bedecked with soft, colourful armchairs and sofas of wicker and ebony. The walls are decorated with works by some of Sri Lanka's foremost artists including Laki Senanayake, Saskia Pringers, Ranil Deraniyagala and Jaya Wirasinghe. Mrs Tennekoon's extensive travels during the 1950s and 1960s are reflected in an impressive array of trophies that now adorn her house – charcoal Cambodian dragons from Angor Watt, Nepalese silver dishes, Vietnamese footstools, Indian wood carvings, Portuguese dolls and British antique furniture. A flight of parquette steps to the left of the living room wends towards a guest's bedroom with views over the garden. The garden was created from space previously

above Mrs Tennekoon, a close friend of the late Bawa, sits on a wicker and ebony sofa. She recently oversaw the landscaping of the gardens at St Peter's Church, an 18th century Dutch banqueting hall, subsequently converted into a church.

opposite An arched walkway runs down the left side of the property, supporting the new bedroom on the first floor. Mrs Tennekoon's bedroom lies to the left of the French doors, which were salvaged from an old Colombo bank.

occupied by the servants' quarters and is accessible via an arched colonnade to the rear of the living room. A bamboo drape hangs across to prevent rain getting in. Bawa was opposed to any such drape but the inimitable Mrs Tennekoon is insistent that "sometimes it was necessary to go against his wishes!" The back wall of the living room consists of an elaborate fretwork, made by Bawa from a fanlight found at an abandoned *walauwa* (a Sinhalese mansion). On the wall above the pond hangs a large sculpture of a banyan tree by Senanayake.

above The dining room is set in a cool, breezy room off the main living room. A mahogany dining table stands beneath a hanging oil lamp. Works by Sri Lankan artists Jaya Wirasingha and Ranil Deranigala hang on the right wall.

right The main living room has a floor of Ceylon teak. In the foreground, a pair of antique nursing chairs face a pair of British Windsor armchairs. Above the sofa hangs an abstract by Sri Lankan artist, Saskia Pringers. The room is decorated with trophies from Mrs Tennekoon's extensive travels around Asia – silver dishes from Nepal, footstools from Vietnam and wooden dragons from Angkor Watt in Cambodia.

The guest's bedroom doubles up as the house library. Family photographs run between weighty tomes on wildlife in colonial Ceylon, Christian thought and autobiographies of world leaders.

The Long Afternoon
GILES WATERFIELD
ANCIENT MEXICO
SRI LANKA
Lloyd George
PERSIA BRIDGE OF TURQUOISE
ISLAND CEYLON

middle street

Galle Fort was declared a UNESCO World Heritage Site in December 1988. Since then, more than fifty of the Fort's 473 houses have been purchased and restored by non Sri Lankans. In Robert Drummond's capable hands, a 250-year-old Dutch villa has been spectacularly restored. The project was privately funded, met all UNESCO's requirements and stands as a terrific example of how such a restoration should be carried out.

Built for a Dutch merchant family in the mid 18th century, Drummond's villa was in a dark and sorry condition when he first acquired it in 1998. A collapsed roof had caused considerable damage to the interior although, remarkably, the original sand and coral walls remained firm.

In setting out to restore the villas, Drummond's principal aim was to modernise the interior while maintaining an emphasis on the original skeleton, the thick walls, arches and hearthstones. All surviving doors and windows were also to be retained so as to keep a sense of continuity.

One of the most striking aspects of Drummond's restoration is the floor. Like many villas in the Fort, this had previously consisted of little more than mud with broken concrete on top. Drummond had the floor levelled and then, using a concrete base, poured a thin coat of samara coloured cement over the entirety. Copper compression strips were added as the cement dried, creating a handsome tile effect as well as acting to prevent any cracks. In certain areas, such as outside bathrooms, the cement was deliberately picked in order to give it a better grip. An added bonus during this process was the discovery of a granite hearthstone between two doorways which now serves as a major floor-level feature. The overall effect has greatly brightened the general ambience.

The removal of unnecessary 20th century partitions and a false low ceiling from the ground floor revealed what was once a large living room and dining area. Three arches on the room's northern side opened out onto an unruly courtyard, overgrown and full of junk. Drummond realigned the arches so that the middle one now stands dead centre between the front door and a frangipani tree in the courtyard. A set of antique doors was then installed in each archway. A contemporary roof was under-laid with planks of cheerful palu wood to create a new ceiling. Skylights were also added, further accentuating the sense of freedom and space.

The street-side exterior has been left unpainted, a useful camouflage on a street of unpainted villas. An inner

above The exterior of the villa's streetside facade features revolving timber windows installed in the late 19th century.
opposite The living room retains a cool and stimulating ambience through the various whites of walls and a Dutch VOC bench from Java. Tilac of Bentota made the white "Barcelona" armchairs while a table of copper strips and steel frame came from Indonesia. From here, three white arches lead out to the courtyard and garden pond.

verandah or *stoep* runs almost eighteen metres in length down the building but gives little indication of the exceptional renovation that has taken place inside. Doors to the left and right of the entrance hall lead into two downstairs bedrooms. Both rooms are now dominated by a low, free-standing cement wall, concealing bathrooms. The wall is a compromise, keeping the integrity of the bedroom whilst simultaneously giving the bathroom an unobtrusive, albeit illusional, sense of space.

Throughout the house, Drummond has been careful to retain whatever original fixtures he could. Windows, shutters and doors – submerged in a century of insensitive paint – have been scraped back to their original state, resulting in a collage of speckled colours.

Aside from landscaping the courtyard into a pool-garden, Drummond's final undertaking was to furnish the house. The bedrooms are simply decorated; visitors tend to relax in the living room and garden. Furniture consists of a rough and ready cupboard made in Bentota using window frames and other salvaged timber goods. But it is in the simple, uncluttered, calming main room that he has truly excelled. The dining table is a particular triumph. A hefty board of palmyra wood is elevated on two cubes of steel. The application of a blowtorch to the inside surface of the cubes resulted in a delightful oil patina on the exterior. Such innovative attention to detail is to be greatly admired.

The villas in Galle were ostensibly designed as shelters but often, as with here, there is an inner gallery or outer room leading straight to an open courtyard or garden. Natural ventilation is essential because of the high temperatures and humidity. The pool is rimmed with stones from the Ratnapura gem mines. The turquoise terrazzo tiles give the pool a stunning golden hue by night.

above Facing out to Middle Street, an inner verandah or *stoep* runs the entire width of the house. The original shutters, doorframes and windows have been stripped back to expose the various paint applications of the past.

right Designed at the Bentota Workshop, a palmyra dining table is elevated on steel cubes. The application of a blowtorch to the inside of the cubes resulted in a delightful oil patina on the exterior. On the walls, modern art from the owner's private collection contrasts with antique Sinhalese tea drying machinery.

above One of two guest bedrooms, equipped with individual contemporary open-air bathrooms, flanking the main entrance. The bedroom doors have been stripped back to their basics and are left at their most rudimentary. Simple white linen and bedspreads lend an uncomplicated feel.

opposite Sun-loungers surmount the upstairs balcony, carefully positioned to catch the evening light. The terracotta tiled roofs of Galle Fort roll into the distance with the New Oriental Hotel and the Clock Tower to the fore. Bamboo blinds are in position to block the sun when it becomes too intense.

doornberg

Arguably the most elegant villa in Galle, Doornberg is also the oldest. According to a bold relief carved on the stone steps of the Dutch colonial homestead, the building dates back to 1712. Substantially extended in the 1850s and again in 2002, Doornberg's latest incarnation places it at the forefront of Sri Lanka's most desirable places to stay in the 21st century.

There has always been something deeply alluring about colonial architecture. Maybe this is simply the fusion of European styles and native traditions. Or perhaps there is something peculiarly romantic about buildings erected in an age when so much of the world was unknown. Either way, constructed in the earliest days of Eurasian commerce, Doornberg remains a remarkable symbol of a remarkable era.

"It was a terrible mess when I first saw it," says Mary McIntrye, the Californian designer who oversaw the building's immaculate renovation. Doornberg had been used as an orphanage by the Anglican Church during the 1950s and 1960s but was subsequently abandoned. When McIntyre first began resurrecting the downtrodden architectural gem in 2001, the garden had returned to jungle and was desperately encroaching upon the house itself.

Stripping back the tar and paint-covered woodwork of the doors and windows was a particularly time-consuming process. "A quarter of a door would take two men with scrapers the best part of two weeks. Eventually we opted for a caustic soda mix to get rid of the tar. We had to be very careful but I think it came out great and it was really very uplifting to uncover all the original mouldings." The cement floor also had to go. Gentle prodding revealed the broken remains of an earlier terracotta tiled floor. Fresh tiles were considered but Mary's initial hesitations soon evolved into a conviction that a terracotta floor would do nothing to brighten up what was, by nature, a typically dark and austere Dutch interior. Thus the floor today is composed of smooth, pale tinted cement slabs, polished weekly and edged with thin strips of glass. The effect is smooth and cheerful.

Although she has been unable to establish the original architect's identity, McIntyre was determined to keep the spirit of the original building. The Dutch architect was

above An engraving on the front step dates the original block to 1712, midway through the Dutch occupation of the island. The formal entrance is in colonial Dutch style, flanked by bedrooms leading to a magnificent hall that is in turn flanked by bedrooms. A 1939 Rover Coupe was acquired by the present owner along with the house.

opposite Verandahs and colonnades are highly practical attributes for tropical houses, affording shade from the sun, fresh circulating air and a sense of internal security. A table is set for tea on the verandah; the nearby cabinet animated by voluptuous urns and bunches of bananas. Against the back wall is an astrological work by the Sri Lankan artist Saskia Pringiers.

"clearly a man of great taste who wanted to produce a building of the utmost quality." That Doornberg remains standing nearly 300 years later is fine testament to his abilities. "The man was a genius," continues McIntyre. "Every room is methodically accurate, right down to the very last centimetre. Even the location is incredible. It's pitched on the hillside at just the right angle to pick up a breeze from both the ocean and the land which is an amazingly helpful thing in those hot humid months."

above At the western edge of the property, a croquet pitch drops down to a stunning L-shaped infinity pool, added in 2001. The pool itself then plunges six metres down into the jungle.

opposite The original architect of Doornberg had a mariner's intricate understanding of sunlight. As the sun sets over the central courtyard, the light of evening gives the house a golden hue. The courtyard features squares of grass, pebble and stone, where guests take their meals and recline in the breeze.

above left The living room leads into one of the original bedrooms. In the Tropics, heat dictates the daily routine. People rise with the sun at 7am and most are back in bed by 10pm. The fabrics were mostly brought from India and form part of the Taprobane Collection.

above right A generous ledge running along the window heightens the spaciousness of the bathroom.

opposite A distressed glass top table augments the sense of history. The brass rubbing to the rear was made by the owner when he was a schoolboy and depicts the Anglo-Norman crusader, Sir John d'Abernon. The door to the left leads out past the pantry to the colonnaded verandah. A model clipper ship made of teak stands in the foreground.

THE GLORY OF THE GOLDEN AGE

10 leyn baan street

Jack and Jo Eden have been keeping a close eye on properties in Galle Fort since they first visited in 1997. In 1999 they acquired a villa on the Fort's Pedlar Street and restored it to such acclaim that friends from overseas were swiftly inspired to do the same. The business expanded beyond the Fort walls and the Edens now manage or market upwards of twenty top-end villas along the south west coast.

One of the hazards of owning a villa in a stunning location like Galle is that one is rarely free of visitors from afar. In the Eden's case, the numbers were multiplied because their business depended on luring people to the Fort. And, in those early days at any rate, where else was there to stay? In their first two years at Pedlar Street, the Edens registered 326 visitors in their guest book. The villa was an elegant two-storey property with much charisma but somewhat lacking in spatial freedom. It's original purpose was to serve as a weekend retreat, not as a principal home. Claustrophobia was wont to set in, particularly during the hotter months. "We feel we will stay in Sri Lanka forever but we needed to get somewhere that we could all call home and in which we felt comfortable raising our children (Maddy and Nico)."

In March 2003, a particularly run-down villa came on the market. Built in the early 18th century as a private residence for the Dutch military commander in Galle, the villa had ultimately come into the possession of a Muslim family living in Colombo. The villa was situated on Leyn Baan Street in the Court Square, a former Islamic quarter now populated by lawyers and magistrates working in the nearby courts.

At first glance, the property was not enchanting. "It looked like a bomb site," recalls Jo Eden. The principal building was used for mushroom storage, most of the fungi having long ago rotted onto the mud floor. Mounds of overgrown rubbish and rubble ran the length of the property, culminating in a derelict shack.

Restoration began the instant planning permission was granted in December 2003. Any work likely to cause noise had to be conducted by night, lest the nearby court proceedings be disrupted by pneumatic drills and such like. As the debris was removed, so the villa's antiquity began to reveal itself – shards of porcelain, old green schnapps bottles and a hefty lead cannonball emerged from the mud.

The 18th century structure remains largely unchanged,

above The house is accessed through an antique Indian temple door leading off Leyn Baan Street. Buddhist stupas are recessed into alcoves by the front door.
opposite Unlike many Sri Lankan homes, the Edens' kitchen is given pride of place as the central room of the house. Resin-coated railway sleepers are employed as a counter-top. Colourful cushions and leather Moroccan "pouffs" imbibe the room with freshness and vitality. A dreamy oil painting of three women by a local artist stands out against the bright samara walls. A Bali-inspired bamboo and Javanese divan further enhances the cheerful ambience. Jakwood shutters from an abandoned plantation bungalow serve as doors to the store cupboard.

above The family sitting room follows an oriental theme, taking as its cue Hong Kong, the city in which Jo Eden was raised. On the right hand wall hangs an abstract painting of the Hong Kong handover commissioned by Jack as a gift for his wife. The armchairs, sofas and black lacquered wedding chest also came from the Eden's townhouse in Hong Kong. A stepladder leads up to a mezzanine floor containing the family's book collection.

right down to the doors and window frames, stripped back to their original natural colour. The roof was replaced with a Javanese inspired bamboo ceiling, set beneath a thin sheet of protective cement and capped with terracotta tiles. A convincing mock-tile floor of egg-white cement was poured upon the mud floor, creating instant sophistication.

A modest doorway on the side of Leyn Baan Street leads into a vaulted hallway bedecked with portraits of Jack Eden's forbears. His great uncle Sir Anthony Eden was Prime Minister of Britain; another ancestor, Lord Auckland, was Governor General of India in the early 1850s. A self-portrait by Sir Timothy Eden, Jack's grandfather, has inspired many Sri Lankan friends to murmur with raised eyebrows at the darkness of the man's complexion. The hall leads directly into a wide, high ceiling kitchen – unusual for Sri Lankan homes where kitchens are often tucked discreetly to one side. A coat of samara brings out the imperfections of the otherwise untouched kitchen walls. Resin-coated railway sleepers are reincarnated as counter-tops and crockery cupboards. Colourful works by local artists adorn the wall casting a buoyant, uplifting spirit upon the room. To the right of the kitchen, a simple living room, a sanctuary of books and board games.

Double-doors in both the kitchen and living room open onto a spacious courtyard of flourishing but controlled vegetation. Verandahs of trellised colonnades run down either side of the yard, the fretwork inspired by the Kasbahs of Morocco. To the left is the dining area with a mural by Spanish artist, Nuria Lamsdorff. An outdoor shower is concealed behind its farthermost wall. To the right, a two storey extension with the children's imaginatively painted bedrooms below and the Eden's master bedroom above. After so many years of entertaining house guests, the Edens are now delighted to say they no longer have a guests' bedroom. "The house is totally designed around us and how we like to live." When friends come to visit, they rent a nearby villa.

above Beneath a brick water-tower on the upper floor, a purpose-built seating area catches the sun throughout the day and provides exceptional views of Galle, taking in the rooftops of the 19th century cinnamon factories and the Old Dutch Gate.

above Looking from the bathroom through a lattice doorway from Northern India to the teak floor of the master bedroom. The mirror is part of an antique Indonesian bed head: the purple armchair came from the Côte d'Azur.

right The Javanese bed is draped in Indian bedspreads and netting fringed with green silk. Table-lamps from Hong Kong stand either side of the bed. The bathroom lies through an elaborate latticework open doorway to the rear.

above The Javanese dining table and chairs are set in an open-air space to the left of the courtyard. Between the colonnades, breezy Moroccan-style arches of teak lend sophistication and natural colour to the environment. Works by Sri Lankan artists Saskia Pringers and Anoma Wijewardene hang either side of an outdoor shower.

opposite The far right side of the villa consists of two storeys. The children's rooms are on the lower floor, connected by an arched colonnaded walkway. The master bedroom lies directly above, its doors opening into the morning sunlight. The black railings on the upper floor were inspired by the Kasbahs of Morocco's Atlas Mountains.

the beach house ▪ taprobane island ▪ the last house ▪ apa villa
victoria ▪ 87 bentota ▪ taru villas ▪ the lighthouse hotel

coastal villas

In Sinhalese legends, the sea is hailed for its celestial powers. It is given a prominent role in the hierarchy of elements, perhaps as the engine room of nature, perhaps as the inspiration for creative thought or perhaps as the prophet of a great and terrible sorrow. That the voice of the sea speaks to the soul is accepted by one and all. In Sri Lanka, an island encircled by ocean, the soul cannot help but respond to such overwhelming power with serene ambivalence.

From the Portuguese villas of Jaffna in the north to the Dutch Fort of Galle in the southwest, the Sri Lankan coastline wends its way around more than a thousand miles of sandy beaches, mangrove swamps, bird-filled wetlands, ambling peninsulas and turquoise bays. The warm waters of the Indian Ocean, sometimes inhospitable, sometimes at ease, rumble into the interminable beyond. In the south, the shore is fringed with coral reefs and small islands; sunken merchant ships from long-gone days rest deep beneath the surface. Majestic ocean liners and tankards ply the distant waters, their colossal bulks silhouetted as the sun sinks to sleep. Surfers speed upon the white-crested barrel waves of Arugum Bay. In Galle, stilt fishermen clamber upon poles securely set into the bedrock of the water and cast a hopeful line.

The south west coast has become so popular over the past twenty years it is now known as the "Serendib Riviera". Hotels and guesthouses run the course of the strip, some bold and demanding, others discreet and intimate.

At Bentota, two hours south of Colombo, one of the most enchanting beaches in Asia provides the setting for two distinguished villas – one an imaginatively renovated 18th century complex by Geoffrey Bawa, the other a contemporary boutique hotel by one of Colombo's foremost designers. The beach at Thalpe plays host to two striking modern villas – Victoria and Apa Villa while closer to Galle, Bawa's Lighthouse Hotel is surely one of Sri Lanka's greatest 20th century architectural triumphs. Many of Sri Lanka's coastal villas are designed as virtual extensions of the ocean. At the Lighthouse, Bawa goes so far as to specifically employ the ocean as a principal feature of the design, insisting guests confront the temperamental waters crashing beneath. Elsewhere, infinity pools appear to plunge directly into the frothy surf while, hung between misshapen coconut trees, hammocks tease the ocean with their gentle sway.

Further east at Weligama Bay, an enigmatic 1920s folly makes for an eccentric yet endearing island retreat. Bawa's influence again makes itself felt along the white sandy beaches of Tangalle – at the late American artist Douglas Johnson's hideaway and at Mahawella, the last private house Bawa designed before his death.

the beach house

In 1993, the American artist Douglas Johnson purchased a small bungalow at Seenimodera, a charming beach just east of Tangalle. Palliyagurugewatte, the original name for the house, loosely translates as "The Vicar's Garden", in reference to an English clergyman who owned the surrounding land during the 19th century.

The bungalow – a well built structure with rudimentary servant's quarters and a small shack for the electricity generator – was built in 1984 as a holiday home for a Swiss restaurateur based in London, but was abandoned during the late 1980s. When Johnson acquired it, the house was almost entirely unfurnished and the interior walls painted a gloomy brown. Moreover, there was no running water, and little garden to speak of, just a wire and bamboo-slat fence at one end of the property.

Johnson was a man of tremendous energy and creative imagination. The Michigan-born artist already had considerable experience in the field of restoration and swiftly began applying his expertise to the "Beach House", purchasing furniture from antique dealers on the west coast, replacing the shutters and repainting the entire house. The principal bungalow now consists of four double bedrooms, a kitchen and an enclosed living room. Cool, white tile floors invite a barefoot lifestyle while, in the bedrooms, large windows, high-beamed ceilings and antique four-poster beds exude a stylish homeliness. Dark wooden furniture, principally Dutch colonial, is offset against an interior of muted maritime greys, blues, creams and white walls. The master bedroom lies on the west side of the building and features an open-air bathroom running down to the pool. Following advice from Bawa, Johnson had the generator shack converted into a detached bedroom, the "Blue House", with its own porch and bathroom.

As the house took shape, so Johnson felt a strong desire to start working in Sri Lanka. For this he needed a studio. Bawa once again pulled out his drawing board, but tragically, Johnson became ill and died in 1998 before the studio could be completed. The present owner, Geoffrey Dobbs, purchased the property in 2001 and has converted the studio to serve as a second detached bedroom.

Dobbs retained much of Johnson's original décor such as his antique furniture, book collection, shell mosaic mirrors and oblique collages and the villa is now one of the south coast's most sought after places to stay.

above The Beach House lies secluded among coconut palms on a stunning white beach near Tangalle on the island's south coast. Formerly the retreat of American artist Douglas Johnson, the bungalow has recently been renovated to critical acclaim.

opposite above Much of the interior artifacts in the Beach House were purchased in Ambalangoda, a village well known for its antiques and puppet making. Here, old butter-making utensils merge with glass fishing buoys and handsome wicker chairs.

below The main verandah follows the eastern sides of the house. The design favours a subtle maritime theme, juxtaposing coral and shell mosaics with the soft blues and muted greys of lampshades, furniture and skirting boards. The chairs and dining table were acquired from Ambalangoda. Antlers from a discarded hunting trophy are reworked into a coffee table. Against the far wall, an oval window of wood, formerly part of a Buddhist temple.

above A long shot of the living room. The dark Dutch colonial furniture and cool terracotta floor of the main living room are effectively lightened by a series of maritime maps, quirky ornaments and collages by former owner Douglas Johnson. Above the rafters, deer trophies recall the property's colonial past. Natural ventilation is essential because of the high temperatures and humidity. Here fresh sea air percolates through latticed shafts above the doors

below The master bedroom continues the aquatic theme with coral ornamentation and shell mosaic mirrors to the right of a splendid French four-poster bed. The bedside lamps were made locally and feature metal shades upon wooden bases. The room looks directly out across the sea and catches the sun from early dawn to the break of dusk.

right The owner designed the bathroom for the master bedroom so its occupants can choose between an indoor shower or outdoor bath. A stone floor guarantees coolness underfoot. Javanese bamboo towel rails are considered essential to any "Asian" minimalist bathroom. A door to the left of the bathtub leads out to the swimming pool.

left Sri Lankan architect Geoffrey Bawa originally designed this building as a studio for Douglas Johnson. Subsequently converted into a bedroom-bathroom outhouse directly behind the swimming pool, the building is much enhanced by an old colonial Dutch door purchased in Ambalangoda. A stately palm tree has been incorporated into the concrete patio to the front of the building.
below One of the two separate outhouse bedrooms at the Beach House where guests can relax on their own front terrace and behold the Indian Ocean. The ever-changing colours of the sea are reflected in several different shades of blue, such as the rehabilitated outdoor table and chairs. By night the room is lit by a fisherman's hanging lamp.

above The flowers of the sea. A close-up of a coral reef bowl set upon a beautifully distressed, pale blue table.
opposite The swimming pool is shaded from breaking daylight by surrounding coconut trees. The owner was anxious to preserve the coconut trees and hence the pool's unusual shape. "I tend to see the pool as part of the garden rather than something that is just a swimming pool."

taprobane island

At a speech in Dhaka in 1985, Geoffrey Bawa observed: "Everything is at the same level; if the world were only flat, you'd see Africa on the horizon." Similar thoughts must have occurred to Maurice de Mauny Talvande fifty years earlier when he purchased a small island in Weligama Bay, almost two hundred metres off the south coast of Sri Lanka. The self-styled Count de Mauny, a charismatic rogue born in Le Mans in 1866, fled Europe amid a whirl of scandals on the eve of the First World War, staying in Ceylon with the tea magnate, Sir Thomas Lipton. Further lengthy visits occurred periodically during and after the war and, by 1920, he had an address at Cinnamon Gardens in Colombo. In 1922 he purchased the future Taprobane Island for a mere 250 rupees and began constructing the neo-Palladian villa shortly afterwards. He described his first encounter with the island in his book, *The Gardens of Taprobane*.

"Shall I ever forget that morning in September when, quite by chance, I first saw Weligama Bay, and in the centre of it the red granite rock, covered with pink and jungle scrub, rising from the Indian Ocean: an emerald in a setting of coral pink. I swam across the narrow strait, scrambled over rocks and briars, and reached the top of the rock. The view from here was admirable. Below me was the Bay outspreading its long arms towards the ocean, until they were lost in the far distance. The coral reefs, sparkling with the diamonds of the spray; the sea, turquoise blue, streaked with amethyst-purple. Beyond, far beyond, the bare horizon; there was nothing between me and the South Pole."

The two-acre island is only accessed via the sea. At high tide one is obliged to wade through waist deep water; otherwise it is a soft walk on white sand. The villa, now owned by an English businessman Geoffrey Dobbs, is a white, octagonal open-sided pavilion set on the island's pinnacle, with generous verandahs running around all sides. A cavernous entrance hall occupies the north side of the building, with separate doorways leading to the bedrooms, bathrooms, dining room and verandahs. Framed by high, teakwood ceilings, stark white walls and a polished white terrazzo floor, the refreshingly shabby interior resembles a set-piece from a 1930s Roman epic. Furniture of predominantly colonial French origin abounds, from the four-poster jakwood beds to the dining table. On the wall hangs miscellaneous works by artists such as Saskia Pringers.

above Evening falls over Taprobane Island. The Palladian-style villa was originally built in 1922 by the landscape designer, Count de Mauny Talvande. Over the years, those associated with the house have included Robin Maugham, Paul Bowles, and Arthur C. Clarke.

opposite Morning light bathes the living room, the view stretching out across the bare horizon of the Indian Ocean all the way to the South Pole. Hunting trophies from the Hill Country adorn the wall. Smooth white granite floors guarantee softness underfoot.

below Count de Mauny planned the house as a pavilion, centred upon an octagonal hall. Eight separate entrances lead through to the bedrooms, bathrooms, verandahs and terraces, each offering a different view of the unique surroundings. The paintings of Taprobane and the moon are by Sri Lankan artist, Saskia Pringers. Pyramid shaped spaces surmount the doorways, enhancing the breezy ambience of the property.

above left In *The Reefs of Taprobane*, Arthur C. Clarke described the island as "being so peaceful and so completely relaxing … that I managed to escape the tyranny of the typewriter [and] learned to wear a sarong." The collage of women's faces is by the Javanese artist, Putu. The writing desk and glass fronted cabinet are of a typical Ceylon colonial style.

above right One of two glass-fronted buildings, completed in 1997, on the west coast of the island. The aromatic bedroom features a jakwood four-poster bed and simple decoration in the form of local wicker furniture and a rattan rug. A traditional Rajasthani painting on cotton of an exotic elephant recalls the Hindu deity Ganesh, the lord of beginnings, remover of obstacles and patron of scribes.

above Mango, watermelon, passion fruit, pineapple, papaya, lime and bananas are a regular feature of the Sri Lankan breakfast. The table is decorated in classic Sri Lankan style with cutlery, napkins and tablecloths from Elephant Walk in Colombo.

left Breakfast is served on the main verandah looking south across Weligama Bay. Count de Mauny was determined that "nothing would interfere with the panoramic vista" which he strongly believed to be "one of the finest views of its kind in the world."

the last house

At the end of his life, Geoffrey Bawa was still working at the same astounding pace he set when he first gave up law and turned to architecture. Projects such as "The Lighthouse", "Kandelama" and "Blue Surf" hotels absorbed much of his time but he always retained a great passion for the private house.

In 1996 Bawa was approached by Hong Kong based businessman Tim Jacobson and his wife Sarah. The Jacobsons had visited Sri Lanka several times previously and decided to establish a house on the south coast. While staying with the American artist Douglas Johnson at Tangalla's "Beach House", they were alerted to a scrubland property overlooking the beautiful, sandy beach of Mahawella.

The Jacobsons were familiar with Bawa's work from the spectacular Lunaganga country estate in Bentota. Indeed it was the Cinnamon Hill House at Lunaganga that inspired them to commission a simple, clean house suitable for beach side living. Bawa surveyed the site in 1998, producing a design concept shortly before a stroke ended his working career. His principal assistant Channa Daswatta took on the remainder of the project, carrying drawings down the corridor from his office to Bawa's bedroom for nods of approval or rejection. The project was finished in 2001. Bawa managed to make one last visit south to see its realization before his death in May 2003. Tim Jacobson recalls the great architect beaming with pleasure at the result. And indeed Jacobson maintains he and his wife are never more content than when together in the "Last House".

The "Last House" is indeed one of Bawa's greatest works. The villa is approached either across a lawn from Mahawella beach or by escalating a series of steps from the inland side. In either instance, Bawa has deliberately ensured the building reveals itself in gradual stages. The villa effectively revolves around a series of generously proportioned open-air rooms, loosely connected by colonnaded walkways and sensual, grassy courtyards. The cool sea breeze is about as constant as it gets, circulating with ease through carefully designed air channels. Every room offers an alternative view to the ocean, the strong vertical and horizontal angles of the building itself serving as a frame.

Under Sarah Jacobson's discerning eye, the interior combines antique doors and windows with Anglo-Dutch

above Looking straight through the double doors of the outdoor living room, the vivid colours of the drawing room roll out to the rustic walls of the dining room.

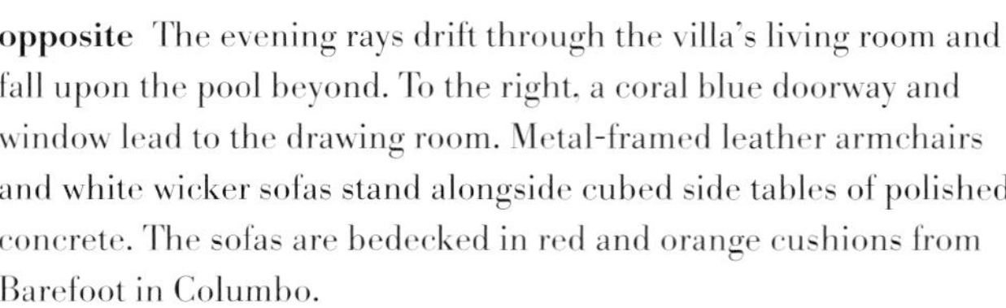

opposite The evening rays drift through the villa's living room and fall upon the pool beyond. To the right, a coral blue doorway and window lead to the drawing room. Metal-framed leather armchairs and white wicker sofas stand alongside cubed side tables of polished concrete. The sofas are bedecked in red and orange cushions from Barefoot in Colombo.

colonial planters' chairs, tea chests, four-poster beds and cast iron bathtubs. However, modern Sri Lankan furnishings are also very much in evidence with, for instance, the cubed cement side tables and butterfly chairs. The contemporary ambience is enhanced by the addition of stunning cement shelving units and worktops in the kitchen and a Philippe Starck style washbasin in the bathroom. The traditional colours of saffron and white walls and grey floors contrast favourably with the more arresting palette of colours used in the cushions. A massive copper-hued tub of polished cement recalls the splendour of Sri Lanka's ancient kings yet simultaneously imbibes the bathroom with a sense of functional modernism. And that is the essence of Bawa's work – a combination of utility and brilliance.

above A prolonged dry spell has taken its toll upon the lawn but summer rains are due to break at any moment. The Indian Ocean rolls south beyond the palms of Mahawella Beach. **left** Completed in 2002, "The Last House" was the last private house built by Sri Lanka's foremost architect Geoffrey Bawa. The two-storey building appears to be elevated upon stilts, providing the lower level with a wide verandah that surrounds a central enclosed drawing room. The sense of space is emphasized in the breezy balconies of the upper floor and a tiled terracotta roof.

above The essence of Sri Lanka is captured by the orange amarillo flowers, aquamarine windows and colourful fruits of the kitchen. Cutlery is stored in wicker baskets to the left of a ceramic belfast sink. A child's dining chair stands against the rear wall of the pantry.

opposite A handsome dyed grey concrete shelving unit in the kitchen contains glassware and crockery.

left The master bedroom stands above the outdoor living room, accessible by four separate doorways leading onto the balcony. Looking through the wooden sliding doors, which span the entire width of the bedroom, beholds the pool and courtyard. A two-tone bedspread compliments the aquamarine doors and latticework.

above A cast iron bathtub dominates the master bathroom, offering views out to the Indian Ocean. The shower and toilet are enigmatically concealed by stable-like partitions. The principal verandah runs past the door.

apa villa

Thalpe beach lies five miles south of Galle Fort on Sri Lanka's coral-strewn southern coast. It is a small and intimate beach; golden sands, palm fringed, turquoise waters, and virtually empty of people. The white-capped waves of the Indian Ocean meander inwards from an interminable distance, the occasional hulk of a liner silhouetted against the skyline. Half-way along the beach, three steps point the way to "Apa Villa", an innovative beach-front villa built by Insight Guides publisher Hans Hoefer in 1996.

The site was previously occupied by a small, rather unseemly Sri Lankan run guest house built in the early 1970s. The original terracotta roof bungalow has now been extensively converted and extended to incorporate four distinct suites, equally distributed between the Cardoman and Saffron Villas. Each suite consists of a generous bedroom with a spacious bathroom to the rear and two sets of double doors leading to a verandah supported by coconut pillars and jakwood beams. Meals are served here throughout the day, many of the ingredients hailing from Hoefer's organic garden at the Illuketia Estate some eight miles inland. The verandah looks directly out across Apa Villa's coconut groves to the sandy beach and ocean beyond. The air is scented with the aroma of heliconia, frangipani and other flowers and spices brought down from Illuketia.

In 1997 Hoefer commissioned Singapore architect Sonny Chan to design a separate courtyard villa on the west side of the Cardoman Villa. This latter building, known as the Saffron Villa, was completed in 1999 with assistance from Australian architect Bruce Fell-Smith. Chan went on to design the acclaimed Tupai House in Bali the following year. Saffron Villa, the largest of the three, stands at the north end of the swimming pool, a rather magical rectangle that always mirrors the colour of the ocean beyond, irrespective of weather or time of day.

It is somewhat exhilarating to know that Hans Hoefer, whose Insight Guide travel series covers 135 countries worldwide, has taken such a keen interest in Sri Lanka. Moreover, he has assumed an intimate role in the decoration of Apa Villa's interiors. Artifacts collected on his global travels now adorn furniture and walls throughout the three villas. In certain areas one can even behold some of his own small, understated works. A complete collection of his Insight Guides is displayed in a library cupboard, surmounted by a catamaran from nearby Koggala Lake.

above Overlooking the beach, a wooden sun-lounger is positioned so its occupant can watch the rolling waves and perhaps spot the occasional sea turtle rising for air. The lounger was made in the Bentota Workshop and consists of three carefully hewn blocks of wood, bound by rope, with Harrison's blue and grey striped cushions.

opposite Saffron Villa is the largest suite and stands at the north end of the pool, a magical rectangle that always mirrors the colour of the ocean beyond, irrespective of the weather or time of day.

Hoefer was assisted in his design by the Swiss carpenter, Rico, who runs the Bentota Workshop on the west coast. He produced a series of steel frame deck chairs and teak sun loungers that now run through the garden towards the sea. Apa Villa's manager, Nikki Harrison, was also on hand to offer her own advice, collected from nearly thirty years in the fashion and textile industry. She created the cool blue and white striped cushions that adorn the various chairs and lounges. She also secured local seamstress Damyanthi Fernando to create cotton bedspreads for the three main bedrooms, each one hand-painted with the spices for which the rooms were named.

opposite Looking from the palm groves towards Saffron Villa, stepping-stones traverse a lily pond and separate the annex into two distinct halves. When weather permits, meals are served on the outside terrace of the villas. Seafood such as lobster, tiger prawn and yellow fin tuna are often the chef's choice. Local tropical fruits like mango, jackfruit, pineapple and passion fruit are also served fresh. In the foreground a white shell-like bowl serves as a footbath for sandy feet.

above The living room features a library containing one copy of each of the Insight Guides, the travel series launched by Apa Villa's owner, Hans Hoefer. A purpose-built set of sleek white concrete pigeon holes against the rear wall also serve to house imaginative sculptures and pots made locally. To the right of the drinks cabinet, a concrete banquette, layered with a navy blue and white striped cushion, runs the length of the drawers. A white-painted wrought iron chandelier hangs from the ceiling.

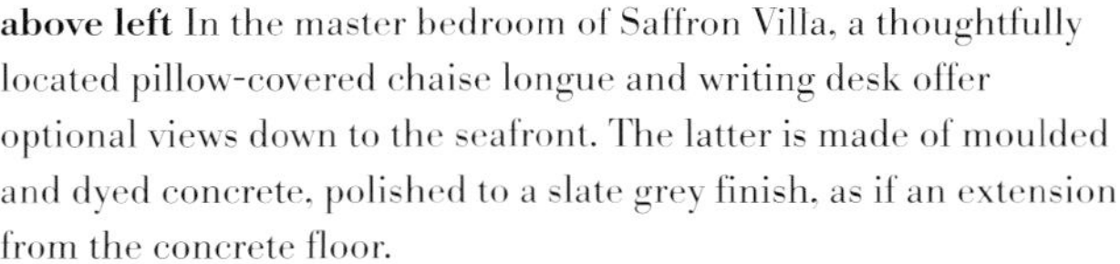

above left In the master bedroom of Saffron Villa, a thoughtfully located pillow-covered chaise longue and writing desk offer optional views down to the seafront. The latter is made of moulded and dyed concrete, polished to a slate grey finish, as if an extension from the concrete floor.

above right The bright, simply decorated bedrooms of Apa Villa feature locally made canopy beds swathed in white cotton and mosquito nets. The cooling onshore wind means there is no need for air conditioning. Here, the master bedroom features a magnificent four-poster bed, the gigantic mattress sunken into the centre of its elevated concrete base. Pillows of leather and canvass surmount a cotton bedspread, hand-painted by Damayanthi Fernando.

opposite Swamped in early morning light, a striking silver-blue swimming pool stretches from the villa towards the Indian Ocean, shaded beneath swaying palm trees; the breaking surf a constant movement upon the vast blue horizon. Decking overlooks the reef-lined beach providing a useful location for sundowner drinks, dining and simple sunbathing.

victoria

Since 1990, the south west coast Sri Lanka has witnessed such an immense boom in up-market property construction that it is now dubbed the "Serendip Riviera". One of the most popular "villas-to-rent" in the area is Victoria, a sprawling coastal bungalow designed by Australian architect Bruce Fell-Smith and completed in 1995. The property lies on the coral beach of Thalpe, five miles south of Galle.

Victoria is a home designed to surprise. One walks through a wooden gateway leading off the main Galle – Colombo road into a small gravelled forecourt of ferns, bamboos and coconut trees. A second inner doorway parts to reveal a fertile water garden, its white walls partially camouflaged beneath aromatic branches of frangipani. The effect is dramatically heightened by an enormous terracotta wall facing the doorway, supported by seven white rectangular columns. Wooden lattice frames have been fitted to the upper parts of the columns. To access the house, one traverses seven inter-spaced granite slabs over a fishpond and then veers either left or right of the giant wall.

Turning the corner around the terracotta wall, it feels like one has stumbled onstage. A massive crescent-shaped sofa occupies the foreground, submerged in cream white pillows. The principal living room is entirely uncluttered, a cut stone floor flanked by colonnaded verandahs of coconut. Along the verandah, open wooden doors and shutters reveal further rooms and vistas. Beyond lies the green of fresh grass, the grey slants of windblown trees and the first glimpses of ocean through columns of coconut palm running down to the beach.

Fell-Smith designed Victoria as a contemporary interpretation of a traditional Sri Lankan courtyard house. The architectural style involves a combination of the many different eras of Sri Lankan history – traditional Kandyan courtyards and open sided rooms merged with subsequent Portuguese, Dutch and British innovations. "Within the context of Sri Lanka history, the Dutch and English left a strong architectural influence and heritage in the Galle area," says Fell-Smith.

Victoria also adopts elements of this history with the use of antique carved panel doors and windows, fretwork panels, giant urns, old granite stone flooring, terracotta roof tiles and timber columns, the latter purchased from a Buddhist Temple auction. All furniture is polished three times a year, first with kerosene and then with a white wax polish. Other elements of tropical architecture such as high

above A tropical rainstorm pounds the south coast, its fall reflected in the saltwater of Victoria's twelve by five metre sunken pool. The Indian Ocean frames the horizon beyond.

opposite Australian architect Bruce Fell-Smith's signature granite walkway rolls across a lily pond to form the principal entrance to the beachside villa. The main body of the property lies behind the white colonnades and the burgundy walls at the rear, accessible from either side of the stepping-stones.

above The giant burgundy wall to the rear serves as an almost theatrical backdrop, underlining the sense of seclusion one feels here. The space is entirely uncluttered, a cut granite floor flanked by wooden doors, folding shutters and views of the surrounding lawns and ocean.

opposite Creamy concrete cushion-covered banquettes are shaped like a crescent moon in the centre of the open-air living room. To the south, the garden and sea beckon one outdoors. Bamboo blinds are in position, ready to be unrolled should the monsoonal rains prove too intense. In the background, the double bed of the master bedroom beckons sleepily in the early evening.

ceilings, open planned spaces and water gardens have influenced the design.

Victoria is a home filled with symmetry – the diagonal thrusts of the floors, the framed views leading to the sea. A twelve metre pool is centrally located to the front of the villa. At the far end of a lawn peppered with windswept coconut trees, a small tiled *ambalama* shelters three sofas in an intimate U-shape, facing directly out to the western seas. To the west may be seen the silhouettes of stilt fishermen. In certain winds, dolphins skim upon the surf. Beyond that, the interminable ends of the ocean stretch to the sky.

LUNUGANGA

opposite The tall timber-planked ceiling imbibes a wonderful regal ambience into the simply decorated master bedroom. Antique rattan chairs and a terracotta floor recall the villa's origins as a coconut plantation in the late 19th century. All furniture is polished three times a year, first with kerosene and then twice with a white wax polish. Four separate double doors lead out to the verandah, bathroom, lawn and drawing room.
right Flowers from the water-garden carry the smells of nature through to the bedroom.

87 bentota

No. 87 Bentota is a secluded country retreat set in a splendid ten-acre garden just off the busy main road between Galle and Colombo. The principal buildings consist of two early 18th century Portuguese style pavilions adapted to serve contemporary needs by Geoffrey Bawa in the late 1970s. The project was commissioned by the Italian sculptress, Lidia Duchini, and her Sri Lankan husband, Dallas Gunasekera. Duchini had worked with Bawa on several previous occasions, most notably when she carved a gold leaf bishop for the Bishop's College in Colombo. The present owner, Rohan Jayakody, acquired the property in 1996, since when he has added his own unique flair.

Initially No. 87 involved two houses, built in 1720 and 1740, facing one another across the main road. The earlier house remains in situ but was rotated by Bawa so it no longer looks onto the road but now faces inland onto the lush garden. The change of orientation was the first major structural adjustment. The walls at the front and back were entirely replaced with sheet glass, enhancing the effect of the antique wooden doors that now seem to almost float. A Cubist influenced staircase was subsequently erected to reach the otherwise inaccessible upper floor, previously a storage space for rice. Walls were removed and a verandah added to the east side, inviting the morning sun to alight the building. Jayakody has now converted this pavilion into an art gallery, displaying an ever-changing exhibit of Sri Lankan photographers and artists. The one constant is a rare collection by Sri Lankan photographer Lionel Wendt on the upper gallery. Amongst the other assorted works on display is a replica of Tui Malila, a Galapagos tortoise presented by Captain Cook to the Tongan royal family in 1777 that lived until 1968.

The 1740 house on the west side of the road was dismantled and rebuilt within the garden at right angles to the first house. All salvageable material, such as the jakwood columns and framed doorways, were carefully reinstalled in the new incarnation. To balance the composition an Italianate pavilion was added just inside the main entrance gate. Finally a high stonewall was erected around the boundary to successfully block out the sound of traffic. The result is an intimate arrangement of three pavilions grouped in a U-shape, beautifully choreographed around a semi-enclosed garden with views running down to a horizon of rice paddys.

Jayakody describes his Bentota estate as "a manicured wilderness". Certainly the landscaped jungle sets the tone for

above top Morning light bursts upon the villa.
above below The exterior of Bawa's second pavilion which houses a further two bedrooms, a verandah, kitchen and dining area.
opposite The present villa incorporates two separate buildings designed by Geoffrey Bawa. The principal living area within the main house features an unusual zigzag stairwell leading to the upper gallery. On a table to the right of the stairs, a replica of Tui Malila, the Queen of Tonga's tortoise, lies encased in a glass pyramid. A doorway to the right leads to the dining area while to the back right, one wanders directly into the Old House gardens.

the entire property. Facing east, the lake-centred garden clearly thrives with the sun's auspicious, early morning glow. By night the silhouettes of mara and banyan trees arise across the skyline, broken occasionally by the various follies erected by the original owner (a ruined chapel), Bawa (a crumbling grotto) and Jayakody (a moon observatory on the lake). The magic of No. 87 comes from a powerful combination of natural synchronicity and human genius.

above A first floor bedroom is simply decorated with contemporary art. A solitary wooden pillar supports a small ledge to create an alcove for a small chest surmounted by a sculpted wooden bust.
left A close up of the stairwell indicates a Cubist influence. A single pillar supports the flight.
opposite The original grain-store has been converted into an art gallery. Here, light floods in through vast glass windows into the upper gallery. At either end, small rooms exhibit works by primarily Sri Lankan artists and photographers such as Lionel Wendt.

overleaf
left The avenue to the original house of 1720 has been converted into a delightful jungle-enclosed swimming pool measuring almost thirty metres in length.
right A secluded dining area in the smaller Bawa building features an oblique blue painted window. Cape bullhorns adorn a stand to the left of a table and pair of chairs.

above A terracotta statue of Madame de Pompadour, found by Bawa on London's Pimlico Road, watches over a pond from behind one of the folly's arches. A contemporary verandah runs in the background.

right Early dawn is dramatically reflected in the lake at the front of the house. A redbrick arch to the rear left beckons towards the principal pavilion.

taru villas

Situated two hours drive south of Colombo, the town of Bentota is widely considered to possess the finest beach on Sri Lanka's west coast. For many years, Sri Lankan designer Nayantara Fonseka and her friends visited Bentota and stayed at a modest guesthouse called Taprobana. By 2001, Fonseka, aka "Taru", was a well-established interiors and fashion designer in Colombo, running a successful event management company on the side. That same year, Taprobana came on the market. "Perhaps it was because of its odd size and shape or maybe because of the countless memories I have of that particular stretch of beach, but I loved the property and could always see its potential." The property was in a miserable condition when Taru duly took on the lease but, by her own admission, "the challenge of converting it into a fantastic small hotel was far too exciting" for her to think of any possible pitfalls. She has since converted the 200-metre long, twenty-five metre wide beachside strip into "Taru Villas", one of Bentota's most prestigious boutique hotels.

Built in the late 1980s, the two-storey villa is reached by a small track leading off the main Colombo – Galle Road. The principal block consists of a well proportioned dining room, kitchen and living area on the ground floor with a polished cement staircase leading to three bedrooms above. A series of open double-doors lead from the main living area directly to the turquoise waters of the swimming pool. Fragrant frangipani and thumbergia blossoms roll along either side of the pool, culminating in an open-sided pavilion with wooden seating arranged for the evening sun. The pavilion serves as an informal border between the pool and the separate "garden bedrooms" on the beach side of the property. At the end of the garden, a modest white gate leads directly over the single track Colombo – Galle railway line to the coconut fringed sands of Bentota Beach.

What sets "Taru Villas" apart is the sophistication of the interior. Taru designed many of the interior fixtures and furnishings herself, such as the sleek steel and teak dining

above The turquoise waters of Taru Villas' swimming pool run west towards the ocean. Fragrant white frangipani and blue thumbergia blossoms roll down the walls of an open-air pavilion separating the pool from the outer bedrooms left of the lawn. The pool shower is a fountain that spouts out of an old granite *sekkuwa* (a primitive mill), carefully positioned beneath a frangipani tree.

opposite Acting as an informal border between the pool and the lawn, the pavilion invites repose against a stylish backdrop of contemporary furniture and smooth polished cement floor. Brass betel nut spittoons are reborn as hanging lamps and ashtrays. Perfume-scented mangrove fruits, called *vatakeyia* in Sinhalese, lend a tropical lilt to the setting. On the wall hangs a reproduction of an old Sri Lankan fresco found in an ancient Royal palace.

chairs, oversized coffee sets, cutlery, menu holders, cement soap dishes and cushion covers. These combine with first-rate reproduction furniture and a floor of cement and cobblestone to create a stylish yet serene ambience. The exterior is painted an almost Tuscan shade of adobe pink, which provides a sensual blush to the poolside area by night. The pink sits comfortably with the more earthy colours of furniture and floor. Boddhistava sculptures, Hindu statuettes and large batik paintings acknowledge the influence of Sri Lanka's ancient past. As such, the villa slowly reveals itself as a significant and successful collage of contemporary and antiquity, unafraid of the past, open to the future.

"Taru Villas" is ideal for the honeymoon couples who make up so many of Sri Lanka's overseas visitors. As such, the staff have evolved an almost Zen-like canny for discretion. They materialize and vanish with grace and decorum. As one dines, looking out to the white-tipped ocean waves, inhaling the aromas of the feast ahead, one's bedroom is subtly converted into a romantic retreat. A deep orange lantern glows softly on either side of the bed, itself a seductive combination of carefully turned cotton sheets, silk cushions and buxom pillows. On the polished cement floor, scattered hints of emerald and slate, flower petals in a waterbowl, a scented candle's flame flirting with the evening breeze that wafts through the open doors of the private verandah.

"Taru Villas" is a two-storey villa built in the 1980s. Looking back towards the house from the pavilion, the bright waters of the swimming pool reflect the surrounding frangipani trees.

left To the left of the lawn, the garden bedrooms lie just a minute's walk from the ocean. Lush tropical ferns, vines, mangroves and halyconias clamber over the walls, providing extra shade for those seeking to relax in the ocean breeze. An overhanging terracotta roof, supported on columns of jakwood, provides shelter for a pair of Indonesian wicker sofa-beds, overlooking a pond.

above Inspired by the Italian-Swiss designer Rico, the original Taru-designed dining tables and chairs were crafted by a local carpenter based in Bentota. The sleek outdoor furniture combines stainless steel frames with strips of *kitul*, an indigenous palm wood. Beyond the balcony, giant coconut trees bend their necks towards the ocean.

above and left The bedheads in Taru Villas are made from a variety of antique windows, lattices, fretwork, doors and cupboards, sourced as individual pieces by Fonseka. The high quality bed linen, bath towels and silk cushions were manufactured locally to Fonseka's designs.

opposite Sunlight pours through the verandah doors of the principal bedroom lending extra cheer as it radiates across an ochre wall directly behind the bed. The silk shaded bedside lamps are made from Fonseka's collection of old betel nut spittoons. Above the traditional Sri Lankan jakwood bed hangs a painting by a local artist depicting a scene from the Karma Sutra.

the lighthouse hotel

A deep, yawning cavern on the south-side of the main Galle – Matara road forms the principal ground floor entrance to the Lighthouse Hotel, one of Geoffrey Bawa's last great architectural triumphs. The hotel was commissioned in 1995 by Herbert Cooray, chairman of the Jetwings travel company. Cooray's father had worked as principal contractor on some of Bawa's earlier projects in the 1960s. The site, overlooking the Indian Ocean, had once been occupied by a magistrate's bungalow but was otherwise a mere extension of a coastline that is constantly weaving around rocky promontories and rugged bays. Under Bawa's guidance, the boulder-strewn landscape was converted into a profoundly stimulating and distinguished hotel.

A doorway to the rear of the entrance hall leads to a vertical drum which confidently spirals upwards through three flights, connecting the principal reception, dining and drinking areas. Sri Lankan artist Laki Sennanayake, a colleague of Bawa's since 1960, was commissioned to create a balustrade running along the inside of the staircase. His remarkable copper and brass creation originated with a drawing he etched in 1961 entitled *The Portuguese Arriving in Ceylon Under a Cloud*. It depicts the battle of Randeniya during which the Portuguese overwhelmed the native Sinhalese, ushering in a century of Portuguese dominance in the island.

The main reception hall occupies the first floor, a vast arena of polished floors and sturdy columns, its southern rim open to the ocean. Such a courteous approach to Sri Lanka's erratic weather pattern fitted with Bawa's adamant belief that all senses should be stimulated by a building's composition. Hence the open-side, which extends to the dining area (the Cinnamon Room), encourages guests to confront the elements to acknowledge the restful beat of breaking waves and inhale the fresh sea air.

To the north of the reception room, another open space directs the way to the principal bedrooms and swimming pools. A grass lawn, dotted with original boulders, is dramatically flanked by two wings running towards a central service block and the pool area beyond. These broad sweeping three storey ranges, enriched by a samara coat, are roofed in Bawa's innovative style; a sheet of corrugated cement overlaid with a single layer of half-round "Portuguese" tiles. Open balconies run the length of each wing, providing access to all bedrooms. Simple elevations between the pillars of the colonnaded walkway

above The soft samara walls of the Lighthouse rise above a canopy of palm trees on the south face. Every bedroom has a private balcony enabling guests to catch the sun and survey the ocean beyond.

opposite In 2003, Channa Daswatta, Bawa's assistant, designed a second swimming pool (25 x 18 metres) and spa for the hotel. To the rear, the Serena Spa continues Bawa's concept through the Moorish colour scheme of red tiles, samara walls and grassy verges.

create a sequence of alternating framed views. No single space is self-contained but rather each runs consecutively into the next, creating a visually invigorating sense of space, whilst simultaneously serving the functional needs of ventilation and accessibility. The overall effect is distinctly Sri Lankan yet dreamily familiar. The Lighthouse has the ability to stir in its guests fragmented memories of a past they never actually witnessed – staggered images of Roman atriums, Moorish souks, Kandyan manor houses and colonial club houses.

At the far end of the residential wings, steps lead down through tropical landscaped gardens to a health spa and swimming pool, designed by Bawa's principal assistant Channa Daswatta in 2003. Just as Bawa invited the elements to cross the threshold into the main reception hall, so his anointed successor teases the ocean by placing the calm, freshwater swimming pool just beyond its grasp.

left Bawa's extraordinary skill in producing concepts at once brilliant and casual is vividly captured in this seemingly "off-the-cuff" exterior. The confident dual tones of the samara wall contrast with red tiles, green grass and a staircase of polished cement. As if to underline the concept, the staircase itself is not a strictly necessary feature. For the roof, Bawa placed a sheet of corrugated cement overlaid with a single layer of half-round "Portuguese" tiles. The process combined the best of both materials, creating a well-insulated, waterproof roof with an attractive old style appearance. Extra tiles were laid at the ridge and eaves to preclude slippage while cement fillets further improved the adhesion.

above left The eastern side of the property tumbles down the palm-fringed coastline. The still waters of the pool stand in stark contrast to the ever-rushing onslaught of the ocean.
above right The original boulders are incorporated as features in the garden court.

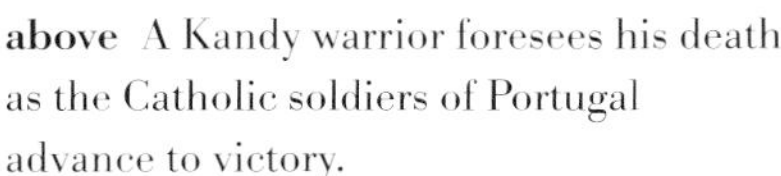

above A Kandy warrior foresees his death as the Catholic soldiers of Portugal advance to victory.

above right A founding member of Colombo's "Young Artists Group", Laki Senanayake, began collaborating with Bawa in 1960, initially as a draughtsman and subsequently as a sculptor. Between May and November 1996, he sculpted this remarkable copper and brass balustrade for the main spiral staircase of the hotel. In 1505, General Lorenzo de Almeida and his Portuguese army were blown off-course while sailing around India. They ultimately anchored in the harbour at Galle. From the flagstone floor, the ensuing battle wends around the inside walls and culminates on the third floor.

right The Sinhala King, demented by the onslaught of doom, sits upon his throne playing upon a flute, just as Emperor Nero fiddled while Rome burned.

opposite The Coat of Arms Bar has a distinctly colonial tone, the ambience of a planters' clubhouse enhanced by a teak floor, billiards table, wicker chairs and Ena de Silva's rich decorative batik ceiling overhead.

above left Bawa's futuristic vision is revealed as an amalgamation of earthy colours and contemporary materials follow a sequence of rigid, inter-connecting lines.

above right A simple open-air staircase leading to the second floor deftly zigzags over the jungle beyond.

opposite Sunlight radiates from the white walls and polished floors of the walkway and sinks into the orange support pillars. Lamps of black wood and stained glass are suspended from the ceiling. The shadows of the colonnaded verandah enhance the sense of geometrical precision Bawa employed as a trademark of his design. Every line seems to edge a different perspective. To the right, a green lawn plunges into the east wing of the hotel.

helga's folly ▪ rafter's retreat ▪ ulpotha ▪ kahanda kanda ▪ illuketia
weeraman walawa ▪ galapita ▪ the river house

▪ jungle & hill country

From the ancient historic kingdom of Kandy to the Victorian tea planter's capital of Nuwara Eliya, Sri Lanka's central highlands have long stirred the soul with their immense beauty. Mountains tumble interminably towards every horizon, some curvaceous and lush, others austere and rugged. Dominating the region is Adam's Peak, a staggering 2224 metre mountain revered by Buddhist, Hindu and Christians alike. The fragrant aroma of tea and spices scents the cool, crisp air. Vast mist-shrouded rivers thunder through wild jungle and carefully controlled plantations of rubber and coconut. Exotic waterfalls cascade down deep ravines and mountain slopes. In the City of Kandy, the last stronghold of the Sinhalese kings, huge crowds gather at the golden roofed "Dalada Maligawa" to behold the sacred Tooth of Lord Buddha, Sri Lanka's most important religious relic. On the hills around Nuwara Eliya, colourful figures pepper the verdant slopes, planting, pruning and harvesting the omnipresent tea bushes, the source of Sri Lanka's foremost export.

With such a fertile climate, Sri Lanka has long been known for its abundance of rice, fruit, vegetables, herbs and spices. From the 16th century onwards, Portuguese and Dutch merchants secured a powerful monopoly on the island's spice and cinnamon trade. After the fall of Kandy in 1815, the British settled the land with Scottish, Irish and English farmers who cleared the highland jungles and planted vast swathes of coffee, cinnamon and coconut. A devastating coffee blight in 1870 encouraged the conversion of these plantations to lucrative cash crops such as tea and rubber. Such crops still grow in impressive quantities, alongside colourful plantations of mango, papaya, banana and pineapple. Over the centuries, recipes from India to England have found their way to the Sri Lankan kitchen, often combined with traditional dishes of rice, seafood and fish.

The insatiable jungle reclaimed many of the colonial plantation villas in the latter decades of the 20th century. The restoration of such structures has now become of prime importance to Sri Lanka's ongoing pledge to preserve its heritage. In Kandy, an art deco chalet (see Helga's Folly) from the 1930s has been sumptuously converted into one of the most outrageous guesthouses in the world. On the south and west coasts, four plantation villas have been stunningly renovated as both boutique hotels and private homes by some of the island's leading designers and artists.

Sri Lanka's commitment to ecological values is also to be found in the following pages with three distinctive jungle communes. In each instance, the simple, time-honoured resources of wood, mud and thatch are woven to create bedrooms, dining rooms, kitchens and drawing rooms. The permanence of these structures is inevitably subject to the weather but diligent maintenance will ensure they have every chance of surviving as long as their bricks and mortar counterparts.

From cluttered mayhem to sheer simplicity, these buildings suggest a unique and charming future for the architectural landscape of Sri Lanka's heartland.

helga's folly

This 1930s guest-house has been redecorated by its owner in a whimsical tropical theme, with decorative pieces and furniture that tell the history of one of the country's most illustrious families.

Helga de Silva Perera Blow is an astonishing lady and proud of it. A daughter of one of Sri Lanka's most prestigious political dynasties, she grew up in a world of colonial teapots, Hollywood gossip and Marxist revolutions. In 1993 she returned from England to live in her childhood home, a 1930s art deco chalet overlooking the ancient city of Kandy. Aided by two student artists, she converted the building into a sumptuous guest house that would serve as an exquisite location should Baz Luhrman ever opt to film *Moulin Rouge: Jungle Style*.

The house, named "Helga's Folly" was blessed with an epic provenance from the outset. Walls are adorned with newspaper clippings, poignant photographs and hastily scribbled verses. They tell how the building was designed by Helga's mother, artist Esme de Silva, a student of the Bauhaus movement in Berlin. Helga's father, Frederick de Silva, is seen shaking hands with Charles de Gaulle. Frederick was the son and heir of political icons George and Agnes de Silva, credited with securing Sri Lankan independence in 1948. A clipping of Helga's aunt Minette de Silva, described as Asia's first female architect, suggests a romance with Le Corbusier. *The Scarlet Pimpernel* is the heading above a shot of Helga's brother Desmond de Silva, a defence lawyer who specialises in aiding Britons in foreign lands to be acquitted from the death penalty. He is married to Princess Katarina of Yugoslavia.

Helga produced another dynasty when, working as a model in London, she married English soldier-historian Jonathan Blow in 1962. She was 17; he was 42. Their progeny were fashion designer Selina Blow and art gallery owner Detmar Blow, who is married to Isabella Blow, the eccentric talent-spotter credited with discovering Philip Treacy, Alexander McQueen, Honor Fraser and Sophie Dahl.

Visitors are taken aback when they first step inside Helga's Folly. The building is enormous, with about forty rooms linked by random staircases and narrow corridors. When Helga grew up here, Esme de Silva's original house had been converted into The Chalet – "a rather grim and ghastly hotel" and a popular stopover for tourist buses to Kandy's famous Temple of the Tooth.

Now, barely an inch of the structure has been left untouched by Helga. Each room is an explosion of

above Every room at Helga's Folly is distinct whether it is the various rooms downstairs or the bedrooms upstairs. Here, local Sinhalese ceramics and dripping candles adorn the blue sponge-washed walls of the dining room. Through the arch another of the exotic dining areas can be seen.

opposite No part of the property has escaped Helga's touch. Drooping candelabras, Christmas baubles, lime green lampshades and multi-coloured party crackers hang from the ceiling of the upstairs dining area.

Fabulously pregnant

flamboyant colours, rich fabrics and gaudy furnishings. The signs of the zodiac beam down from ceilings; Sri Lankan art adorns the walls; satin curtains tumble from ochre staircases; stag heads, peacocks and antique weaponry clamber up Brahminesque blue-washed walls. It's a jungle scheme, reflected in carefully placed mirrors, some gilt-edged, others shrouded by Gothic candelabras. The arrangement of furniture and objects emphasises "the whimsy of life", and reflects Helga's preference to juxtapose and "mix the pedigrees". Much of the furniture is antique Sinhalese or inherited heirlooms of the de Silva family, while decorative pieces throughout are from local markets and toy shops.

opposite Two household staff are seated on an 18th century Portuguese sofa. Their red cotton saris were specifically designed by Helga. On the wall are family photos and a mural by Sri Lankan artist Kolibuwilla depicting the British siege of Kandy in 1815. Local Sinhalese weavers wove the carpet.

above left The Le Corbusier Room stands opposite the Dove Room and features late 19th century chairs and a Le Corbusier style sofa by Esme de Silva. The silver leaf screen was a gift to George de Silva from the Chinese Emperor in 1910.

above right Situated on the second floor, the Dove Room is one several upper storey rooms that look down upon the great Kandy Lake. The eponymous dove tree was painted by Kolibuwilla and is accentuated by festive lights hung in its imaginary branches. The glass vase is hand-blown Venetian by Mirano. Helga created the silk sari curtains. On the left, a planter's chair with moveable arms designed during the late 19th century.

"It took us three months," says Helga, sweeping through the house in Jackie O-style shades and flowing velvet red robes, a pair of Dalmatians at her heels. "I had two art students come and stay and we went for it with whatever came to hand. When the brushes wore out, we used sponges. When they went, we started with pieces of cloth. It was tremendous fun."

In the visitor's book, everyone searches for an adequate description. "Where Alice in Wonderland met the Marquis de Sade" is one. "Soft pornography," suggests another. Carl Muller was perhaps closest when he wrote: "Truly, the gods of music, art and drama have created the impossible."

"This houses is always evolving," says Helga. "Like top-seed, it keeps on growing. I hope I have given back some of the soul of the building."

Breakfast is served in The Red Room on the second floor. This sumptuous room is an unusual colonial Asian hybrid. The cabinet is 19th century Sinhalese, the silver wine goblets from Britain, the tiles from Colombo and the wall-puppets from Rajasthan. The checkered black and white floor contrasts auspiciously with the zodiac paintings on the ceiling.

MODLIA

left Caricatures of Helga's legal forbears chalked by herself and completed by Sri Lankan artist Kolubowilla adorn the library walls. A silver slipper doubles as a doorstop. The basket house on the bookcase was woven for a fancy dress ball in Kandy in 1995.
below left A hitherto "rather plain" wall is jollified by this rather irreverent scene, chalked by Helga and completed by local artist, Lesley Jayawardane.

below The Drawing Room is decorated in a cheerful jumble of colours, antique furniture from the family estate, baroque candlesticks, Christmas baubles and ornaments purchased at local markets. In the rear, a stairwell rises to the second floor, its walls covered with newspaper cuttings and photos illustrating the de Silva family's remarkable past.

opposite The principal Drawing Room is on the ground floor. its walls adorned with ceremonial spears and sculpted game heads. Double doors to the left lead down to the gardens and the jungle beyond. Helga made the cushions with local sari silk. The painting above the 18th century Sinhalese cupboard is in the style of Italian artist Fornasetti.

rafter's retreat

Channa Perera's innate calmness probably stems from his past career as a mariner. For two decades, he worked as an engineer on the hulking cargo ships that travelled to and fro across the world's oceans. He speaks intimately of Panama and the Ukraine, Southampton and Taiwan. But eventually he grew bored with the interminable waters and returned home to take on the family estate in Sri Lanka. The estate was centred upon a large elegant white walled, red roofed two story *walauwa* built by his grandfather, M.G. Perera, in the early years of the 20th century. M.G.P., as he was known, was a Sinhalese Catholic with a Portuguese name who came east from Colombo and purchased a 2000-acre property on the banks of the River Kelani outside Kitugala. He then developed the property as a rubber and tea plantation, effectively providing employment for all the labourers in the area. In due course, M.G.P. rose to become *Mohandirum* (Mayor) of the district. Channa never knew his grandfather, who died in 1932, but he remembered coming here often as a child to visit his grandmother. There is certainly a sense of history about the building, odd for something so relatively young. The past is shaped by stunning antique furniture, family portraits, leaf tables, the beautiful, dust covered porcelain and the Buddhist "svastika" engraved veranda from which M.G.P. once addressed the masses below.

Channa confesses he always found the *walauwa* a little too foreboding. The cold portraits of his tribal elders, the strict walls and cane blinds, the sheer emptiness of the building. He preferred the river. Life in this area is utterly dictated by the pace of the Kelani, sometimes a parched stream, once so powerful it rose to cover the steps of the *walauwa*. Less than a mile upriver, David Lean filmed the wartime epic *The Bridge On the River Kwai*. In 2001, Channa decided to build a cabin made of jungle branches, overlooking the river so that he might sleep to the sound of rushing waters. The "treehouse" was finished in three weeks. During his first night, Channa realized he'd forgotten to build a toilet. Next morning he cut a square in the floor, hammered a ladder together and, over the course of a week, created a bathroom on the lower floor. The room was walled with square stones taken from the estate's long abandoned rubber smoke-house. At the time he ran white water rafting trips and accommodated people in three bedrooms in the *walauwa*. One day, two Australian surfers visited and decided to try a night in the treehouse. Next day they got on the phone and cancelled all further engagements, including a return flight to the Maldives. "It is just a box on a tree," shrugs Channa.

There are now ten of these "tree houses" scattered along the riverbank, shielded by stately jungle trees and connected by a rocky path to the main *ambalama*. This two-tiered wooden building of soft browns, greens and khakis, was converted from M.G.P.'s original stables. The softwood planks on the ground were sanded down and brushed,

above To the rear of the tropical retreat, the *walauwa* was built by the owner's grandfather in 1911 as the centre piece of a once lucrative rubber plantation. The owner confessed himself more at ease with life along the river.

above The principal living area or *ambalama* was formerly the plantation stables. Everything – chairs, blinds, walls, roof beams, staircases, ashtrays – is made from an ingenious mixture of rope and gnarly wood, infusing the area with the dulcet shades of the jungle. The milla-wood columns were recycled from the estate's rubber smoking rooms. A roof of interlaced coconut branches was placed on top. The tables are made of sanded and varnished telecom cable rollers. By night, the *ambalama* is lit by carefully entwined fairy lights and old onion string-bag lampshades from Bombay.

columns of milla-wood were strategically placed, a roof of interlaced coconut branches was fixed on and then the furniture arrived. Three great circular tables made from the disused wooden rollers of telephone cables, a herd of wooden chairs beautifully crafted by Channa from the bark and sides of ginisapu trees, a string of lampshades brilliantly created from the stringbags used to import onions and garlic from Bombay. Fishnets hang above the roof of the building to capture falling durian fruits before damage is done. The saplings of M.G.P.'s original garden now tower overhead – a jambo tree with its bitter red fruits, a ramboutan with its sweet lychee-like offspring, the olive tree which Channa uses to make sweet wine, the beautiful nar tree with its fragrant flowers used for herbal medicines.

Sleep is matchless, the noise of birds, crickets and grasshoppers drowned by the soothing sounds of fresh water rolling over rocks, the Kelani on the eve of the Siberian monsoons, gathering waters from Adam's Peak and all the highlands between, steering its ancient course for the Indian Ocean and the South Pole.

left Built of timber, mud and stone, each hut is named for the predominant wood used. This hut, "Wal Dell", is named for the wild breadfruit employed in its floor and walls, a wood often used for dug-out canoes. Even the table is a simple rack of ginisapu branches. A ceramic water-pot stands on a ledge beside the bed. The double beds are bedecked in white cotton sheets and locally made bedspreads. In the background, the private balcony leans over the River Kelani.

above Rope and junglewood merge to form everything from the balcony railing to the owner's own simple table and chair designs. Roll-down bamboo screens protect against rain and wind during the monsoon season. The green jungle leaves form a canopy overhead.

far left Looking across the Kelani towards "Hora", the frothing waters are a regular haunt for Oriental Dwarf Kingfishers, the Chestnut Brown owlet and other birdlife.
left "Hora" is made of a wood once popular for railway sleepers. Each hut is secluded in its own setting of riverside vegetation. A traditional water bowl with flower petals stands to the left of the steps.
below The huts are scattered along the riverbank, shielded by stately jungle trees and connected by a rocky path. A corrugated iron roof protects the hut from the pendulous branches of a durian fruit tree.

above left The bathroom on the lower floor is accessed through a trapdoor in the bedroom floor above. Jungle leaves are woven into the steps. Even the loo roll holders and chain pulls of the clay-baked toilet are made of jungle wood.
above right A bathroom mirror, bound by olive wood and wedged into the trunk of a jambo tree, reflects the natural run of the wilds.

ulpotha

In 1995, Sri Lankan businessman Viren Perera purchased a ruined manor house set deep within the tropical jungles of central Sri Lanka. A Canadian émigré, Perera was charmed by the provenance of the nine-acre estate, which he had read about in a book by a local teacher. Shortly after, he met Muddiyanse Tennekoon, a farming expert who shared his passion for *puranagama*, the old Sri Lankan system of self-sustaining village life. London ex-pat Giles Scott came on board soon after and Ulpotha was born.

Ulpotha takes its name from the Sinhalese word for "water-spring", a reference to the vast manmade reservoir – or "tank" – built here perhaps two thousand years ago. The tank is located on a stretch of land where hot thermal waters bubble up from beneath the surface. Since 1995, Scott and Perera have converted the south-side of the tank into an upmarket yet highly discreet eco village.

The village is centred upon the original manor or *walauwa*, the first part of the property to be restored. The colours fit flawlessly, soft and natural tones, coral, pale apricot, dark *galgamuwa* green, natural wood, beige. The occasional splash of red brings to mind the adventures of Lord Katargama whose disciples are reputed to have been the first to settle by Ulpotha's tank. An internal courtyard flickers through jackwood window frames, its blue-washed walls recalling the Brahmin houses of Northern India. Yellow umbrellas wait patiently alongside walls, ready for use in rain or sun. Earthenware pots for making oils and medicinal concoctions lie carefully scattered about the place. Hanging reed baskets gently rock in the afternoon breeze. By night the warm glow of oil lamps and candles replaces the harsh light of electrics. Portuguese-style pitch tiling ripples handsomely over the roof.

An *ambalama* was subsequently built on to the *walauwa*; an enchanting open-air timber pavilion lined with vibrantly-coloured cushions. Here guests gather for meals and drinks and sprawl out amongst books and guitars. Days are shaped by earth and water, invigorated by the invisible spirits of the wild, fed by the quality and quantity of the delicious organic meals.

Perera's wish to create a self-sustaining village was welcomed by the small farming community who lived nearby. For centuries they had continued on in the spirit of their forbears, quietly celebrating the passing phases of the moon and uniting whenever their water-logged paddy fields beckoned. In recent years, however, the younger generation had tended to pack their belongings in a headscarf and make the long and deceitful trek to the suburbs of the island's big cities. Since Ulpotha opened to visitors in 1999, many of these local farmers now earn a living through the innovative retreat's twenty-two-acre organic farm.

above According to the legend, traveling mendicants from the Himalayans settled here amid the seven hills surrounding Ulpotha convinced it was the final resting place of Lord Katargama. A shrine dedicated to the deity was subsequently erected at the entrance to the nearby village. During the dry season, water levels become so low that water buffalos come here to graze. To the rear, one of the adobe mudhuts opens east to the morning sun.

left At the heart of Ulpotha is the *ambalama*, an enchanting open-air pavilion where guests gather throughout the day. At meal times a large cream mat of woven palm leaves is unrolled upon the polished wooden floor. Meals are then served on large palm leaf trays. All food is grown at Ulpotha, beautifully presented vegetarian dishes of curry, salad, sambal and fruit. Overhead, colonial style pitch tiling ripples over the *ambalama* roof.
below Ulpotha's native treatment centre (*wedeegedera*) offers herbal steam baths, ayurvedic massages and *panchakarma*, a local treatment involving hot oil dripped onto the forehead.

A dozen adobe mud huts lie scattered down avenues of arekanut palm trees. The huts are open to the elements but guests sleep on beds of wood and reef, cocooned by mosquito nets and drop-down bamboo blinds. The roof consists of palm fronds carefully interwoven with jungle-wood beams. All one's basic needs are catered for. A slender terracotta pot filled with fresh spring water is capped with a coconut shell. A marble bowl of floating lotus petals lies at the foot of the bed. The scent of incense in the night air. The gentle glow of an oil lamp. And maybe, far away, beyond the frogs and cicadas, the distant rumble of the Maho train, a hint of civilization. There is something deeply sacred about Ulpotha. It engulfs you with its ambience.

below left The essence of Ulpotha is *puranagama*, the traditional Sri Lankan system of self-sustaining village life. Under the guidance of Mudiyanse Tennekoon, hundreds of fruit and nut trees have been planted alongside vegetable beds, rice paddys and medicinal herbs. Ulpotha's unique and organic red rice, pictured here in a *bias* (storage bin), is now distributed to farmers throughout the island to be used as seed paddy.

below right Neat avenues of areka nut palm trees, fringed with pretty coconut shells, link the various huts and walkways to the central *ambalama*.

above Parked outside the *wedeegedera*, a bicycle is still the fastest moving vehicle in Ulpotha.
opposite The two-acre lake at Ulpotha lies within one of the oldest inhabited regions in Sri Lanka, a landscape of ruined palaces, crumbling hermitages and venerable bo trees. A nearby rock bears writing that pre-dates Sanskrit.

right The kitchen benefits from five separate fires, each using a distinctive type of wood. This enables the cook to shift between temperatures, whilst simultaneously offering a variety of options for the smoking of food. The colourful flower bedecked sarong worn by the cook is typical of the highland style in this part of Sri Lanka.

left, above and opposite To the right of the *ambalama*, Ulpotha's kitchen (*murtange*) might be no different to that used in these parts thousands of years ago. A cook scours a coconut with a long oblong stone; green lentils lie on a stone board awaiting the chopping knife. Terracotta pots sizzle upon fires of junglewood and coconut shells. From here the dishes are carried through to the *ambalama* and served on large palm leaf mats.

above The original manor house or *walauwa* still operates as the backbone to Ulpotha. The disheveled pea-green walls of this bedroom serve as a pleasing antidote to the chaotic colours of the jungle beyond the windows. The four-poster bed was made in the village using *kohamba*, a local wood renowned for its therapeutic qualities.

left Scattered throughout the cheerful jungle, seven adobe huts serve as the principal guest bedrooms. In the absence of electricity, the wind is enlisted for air-ventilation. The only wall in these huts is behind the bed. The other three sides are open to nature, save for the low sweep of the woven palm-frond roof and the option of drop-down bamboo blinds. The beds are made in the local village, an ingenious fusion of junglewood and rope, cocooned in mosquito nets. Bowls of floating flowers and scented joss add to the tranquility.

kahanda kanda

Although his maternal grandfather owned a substantial tea and rubber plantation near Bentota in the days of British Ceylon, George Cooper did not visit the former colony until 1999. Just four days after his arrival, he purchased a rambling ten-acre tea plantation some six miles inland from the port of Galle. A dilapidated hill-top *walauwa* crowned the property, its views encompassing the surrounding jungle and Koggala Lake below. The following year Cooper teamed up with Australian architect Bruce Fell-Smith to design a new villa on the site of the *walauwa*. Cooper was determined to create an ambience that would stand in utter contrast to his somewhat hectic life as an interior designer in Gloucestershire. He was also anxious to preserve the existing coconut trees surrounding the property. A decision was made to construct a villa that would gently wallow along the crest of the hill and incorporate the outer world.

Kahanda Kanda, meaning "Yellow Moon Mountain" in Sinhalese, is amongst the most inspired of the new villas to have been built in Sri Lanka. A steep rocky path leads to a set of steps flanked by two walls, one the colour of aubergine, the other of saffron. "Originally I was going to leave the walls white," says Cooper, "but then I decided it might look more welcoming if they were different. The colours represent those worn by Buddhist monks in Sri Lanka – aubergine for the highland monks, saffron for the ones you see in cities." The saffron wall particularly stands out, running some eighty metres in length through the property. Glassless windows are symmetrically placed along the wall offsetting any feeling of aloofness and providing alternative vignettes of the newly planted tea and cinnamon fields that lie beyond.

The principal area of the villa consists of three detached open-air rooms that run adjacent to the southside of the saffron wall. The first is the master bedroom, a simple yet sumptuous room with high ceilings and four separate double door entrances. One of these doors leads east from the bedroom, past a garden pond, to the main drawing room. This stylishly decorated room is imbibed with a distinctly oriental theme, embellished by elaborate windows crafted from old timber egg crates. A polished cement floor and exposed timber ceiling strike a sensual balance between

above From the poolside patio, the main buildings of Kahanda Kanda stretch east in the sinking sun. A stepping stone walkway runs over a lily pond connecting the open-air dining pavilion to the drawing room. In the distance, the master bedroom awaits the fall of night.

opposite The backbone of this spectacular Zen-like villa is an eighty-metre saffron wall, which divides the main area of the property from three jungle enclosed guest suites. Built on ten acres from May 2000, the villa was designed and completed over ten months by Australian architect Bruce Fell-Smith in collaboration with the English interior designer and owner, George Cooper.

contemporary desire and tropical harmony. All sofas, chairs and tables were designed by Cooper and built at The Workshop in Bentota.

Fell-Smith's signature – a series of stepping stones similar to those used at Apa Villa and Victoria – runs across a second garden pond connecting the drawing room with the dining pavilion. Here again the designers' courage is rewarded with a stunning polished teak tabletop set upon two moveable stainless steel cubes. As a dining table, it is sleek and functional, capable of seating sixteen when fully extended. As with the drawing room and the master bedroom, the colour scheme is almost exclusively black and white. The great saffron wall running past the northern doors provides ample cheer, while terracotta pots of fresh orchids merge with the fragrance of the tropics.

To the west of the dining room lies the infinity pool, sedate and alluring, its fresh waters blooming against a dark green polished cement finish. At the far end of the pool, another aubergine wall brackets the edge of the villa, again casting an encouraging hue over its immediate environs. Behind the saffron wall, to the north of the property, three terraced pavilions provide accommodation for eight further guests, each bedroom featuring an open-air bathroom.

The genius of Kahanda Kanda is undoubtedly its architectural layout, a design that unwinds with a near sacred serenity. The dominant colours of the main walls provide the warmth. The geometrical precision of the three main rooms shows a tremendous mastery of utility. And surrounding this magnificent villa, the verdant jungle and tea estate supply the scent and sound that is unmistakably Sri Lanka.

The stylishly decorated drawing room strikes upon a distinctly oriental theme. This is the essence of the owner's desire to find a divine antithesis to his hectic other life in London. The lily ponds either side of the drawing room lend a cool, sedate air to the space. All sofas, tables and chairs were designed by Cooper and made by Sudath Antiques in Balapitiya.

Every part of Kahanda Kanda invites repose. Here, a magnificent fourteen metre banquette, draped in Sri Lankan handloom, runs along the drawing room wall, offering views over the surrounding jungle trees and the lagoon below. A large urn dominates the entrance from the master bedroom on the eastern side.

A contemporary dining table composed of teak with an ebony band around the exterior is set upon cubes of polished stainless steel. The table and chair were made by The Workshop in Bentota. Already the setting has the aura of a thousand successful dinner parties wafting over it.

above left The master bedroom occupies the easternmost part of the villa, blossoming with the morning sun. A freestanding wall directly behind the bed conceals two open-roof bathrooms. A series of double doors and floor-to-ceiling shutters allow the occupants direct access to the drawing room, lily pond, main entrance and gardens.
above right Between the master bedroom and the drawing room, the King of Kandy surveys the property from his lily pond.
opposite Lunch is served in a recessed poolside alcove beneath the shade of a blossoming jak tree. The pool has a dark green polished cement finish.

illuketia

Illuketia is one of the oldest British colonial houses in Sri Lanka. Early 19th century maps suggest the site, located some five miles inland from Galle Fort, was originally developed as a coffee plantation in the 1830s. That decade saw the first real influx of British settlers since the island was seized from the Dutch in the Napoleonic Wars. When a leaf blight destroyed the coffee plantations in the 1870s, the owners rapidly switched to tea, which has been the island's foremost cash crop ever since. The Illuketia plantation, abandoned during the troubled 1960s, was verging on complete ruin when the present owner, Hans Hoefer, first visited the area in 1990. As founder of the Insight Guides, Hoefer's career has given him intimate knowledge of more than 135 countries worldwide. But it was Sri Lanka – and Illuketia in particular – that finally captured his imagination.

The house is set upon a hill in the midst of a magnificent rambling seven-acre garden. Rugged stone steps meander up the lush slopes into a semi-covered courtyard centred on a rectangular fishpond. An open-air balcony above offers a tranquil space for reading and contemplation. Four doors lead from the courtyard to large airy double bedrooms, each with an ensuite bathroom. The master bedroom, The Hibiscus, features its own sumptuous verandah, the view encompassing a fertile horizon of jungle trees and rice paddies. At the far end of the courtyard, a pair of carved antique doors beckons one into Illuketia's magnificent living room. Four giant bamboo sofas sprawl invitingly beneath a pair of Balinese chandeliers hanging from a unique oriental roof. Two red Chinese lacquer cabinets reinforce the Eastern theme. The interior design is the work of Welsh-born Nikki Harrison, who moved to Sri Lanka with her husband Bob thirty years ago.

The antique doors are from a set of nine acquired from an abandoned Buddhist temple and now set into the white-walls of this vast room. The other seven doors open onto a wonderful U-shaped verandah that loops around the entire room. Food and drink are served in five distinctive seating areas around the breezy, shaded verandah. Some gaze out to the waterlogged paddy fields, others behold jackfruit, ginger bushels, heliconias and fruit trees. Throughout the day, the sound of nature echoes around the verandah – rumbling bullfrog, chattering cicada, silver-haired monkey, wild bird.

A series of stepping-stones roll down from the verandah through an arch and into Illuketia's garden. After forty years of abandonment, the original gardens were in a dreadful state when Hoefer purchased the property.

above Dawn breaks over Illuketia to reveal a series of steps leading upwards through the jungle to the main entrance. An open-air balcony on the second floor separates the office from the library and billiards room.

opposite Three arches lead from the courtyard, the main entrance, balcony staircase and master bedroom respectively.

However, a year of hard graft by Bob Harrison and a team of ten gardeners has resulted in one of the more unusual gardens in Sri Lanka. Tropical plants of often gargantuan proportions are compounded by grotesque statuary, mythical follies, bamboo groves, luscious frangipani and a dusky, lotus covered pond. The latter is bordered by another house – the Pond House – with its own separate bedrooms. By the entrance, a patchwork of nursery beds, bordered by railway sleepers, bursting with salad greens and herbs.

After more than 125 years of existence, the Illuketia estate stands as testament to a new era in Sri Lankan history where the colonial ambience of old can merge successfully with the modern desire to escape the anthill and recline amid a tropical fantasia.

opposite left Smooth polished concrete blocks provide the perfect space for double mattresses in bedrooms such as The Lotus Room. A small ledge surrounds the bed. A mosquito net hangs from a metal frame inserted into the ceiling. Simple stylish wicker furniture, colourful flowers, modern art and strong fabrics inspire a sense of tranquility.

opposite right The Hibiscus Room is the master bedroom and features its own balcony and walk-in wardrobe. Bedspreads are patterned and coloured to match the bedroom's name; paintings emulate the vivid colours outdoors.

above Shaded in evening light, the Hibiscus Room has a private verandah. Pillow covered concrete seats look out onto rice paddies while a collection of urns lends an air of mild opulence.

left The fragrance of Illuketia's meandering wildlife floats through the house, constantly lulling one out into the wilds. Simple clay urns and a wicker bed suggest an understated elegance. A sculpture of a sleeping dog asleep on the polished cement floor in the living room further underlines the restful ambience. A mosaic skirting board runs through to the terracotta floor of the verandah beyond.
opposite The living room is accessible by nine carved antique doors from an abandoned temple. Red Chinese lacquer cabinets line the walls between a set of four giant pillow-covered bamboo sofas. Balinese chandeliers hang from the ceiling.

above Stepping-stones run across a small moat surrounding the verandah. A pretty Victorian archway provides access to the rambling seven-acre garden of absurdly shaped palm trees, lotus covered ponds, fragrant frangipanis, lush bamboo groves and vine-covered mangosteens.
At dawn and dusk the lawn and its surrounding trees become the playground of silver-backed leaf monkeys.
left The living room spills out through antique doors onto a large colonnaded verandah where meals and drinks are taken. Metal-framed sun loungers and wicker armchairs invite repose.

weeraman walawa

Saskia Pringiers was born in Belgium in 1945 and worked as Professor of Visual Arts at St Lucas in Ghent before moving to Sri Lanka in the 1980s. Her husband, Pierre, is presently Belgian Consul to Sri Lanka. Regarded as one of the greatest artists currently operating in Sri Lanka, Saskia's work offers a dynamic richness that appeals to those with a more optimistic, vibrant view of human life and the future. Her artistic vocabulary is drawn from several reservoirs: mythology, spirituality and symbolism, introducing an esoteric dimension to her work.

In many ways, Saskia's house in southern Sri Lanka is an extension of her approach to the canvas – an enchanting distillation of traditional values and modern living. The building, a restored 18th century Dutch *walauwa*, lies seven miles north of Weligama Bay. A track wends its way through dense jungle scrub, the verdant skyline occasionally broken by a *dagoba* or a ramshackle bungalow.

Surrounded by coconut groves on its southern flank, the Weeraman Walawa is a two storey building reminiscent of a French chateau. Boisterous roofs of terracotta tiles arch over beautifully panelled balconies and ornate window eaves.

In typical Kandyan style, the building is centred upon an internal courtyard. A hallway of smooth polished concrete runs between the office and Saskia's studio to a resilient white verandah looping around three sides of the courtyard. The fourth, or south side, opens onto a grassy slope rolling up towards an orchard. The verandah is a broad, sweeping affair, bracketed by wooden doorways and carved pillars, furnished with colonial antiquities and giant oil drums.

A checker floored kitchen and expansive dining room occupy the ground level on the east side of the courtyard. Elegant lights of metallic black, designed by Saskia, are suspended above a robust dining table of polished grey cement. To the right, a cantilevered staircase rises to the three guest bedrooms on the upper floor, one a ghostly attic overlooked by a giant communion tapestry.

The two principal bedrooms and main living room lie on the north side of the courtyard, each room accessible through doors from the courtyard verandah. The entrance to the living room is particularly impressive, the doorway surmounted by an elaborate arch. Decoration is minimal – a hybrid of Asian artifacts, archaeological relics, ginger jars,

above Iron seats and sun-loungers, made locally to Saskia's design, are adorned with black and white cushions from Paradise Road in Colombo and carefully positioned by the swimming pool.
opposite Three sets of double doors envelop the main living room and provide access to the verandah looping along the southside of the house. Like Saskia's artwork, which hangs from the walls, the use of black and whites creates an ambience of refined sophistication. Wooden doors and a large granite slab, commandeered as a coffee table, provide a natural contrast.

bullhorns, wicker chairs, orthodox candlesticks and stoneware. A wide white sofa and black day-bed face each other over a granite block table; Saskia's own art adorns the walls. Both bedrooms and the living room have a second, larger double door on their northern flank which provides access to a second colonnaded verandah, the views beholding misshapen palm trees and a swimming pool surrounded by iron sun loungers adorned with black and white cushions from Paradise Road, Colombo. Latticed frames above all doors and windows allows for a constant circulation of fresh air.

above An elaborate plastered arch separates the northern end of the living room from the courtyard. The chest originally belonged to a doctor of ayurvedic medicine and was used to store his various remedies. The inscription above is in French and quotes Mother Theresa of Calcutta: "Give your hands to help and your heart to love."

above The smooth polished concrete floor ambles north along the verandah toward the owner's studio and office. Latticed frames above the doors allow air to drift into the adjoining living room and bedrooms. An old well-stone doubles as a coffee table. Two serpentine elephants stand guard by the living room door. A pair of wicker seats behold the courtyard.

opposite A series of planter chairs and large urns, formerly used for carrying oil, line the verandah, the doors to the left leading into the living room. The checkered cushions are from Paradise Road, Colombo.

left The kitchen runs parallel to the dining room at the east end of the house. The black and white theme of the living room continues in the semi-checkered floor. On the window ledge stand silver pots of herbs and spices.
right A flight of concrete steps leads up from the dining room to the three bedrooms on the east side of the house. In the foreground, a substantial concrete dining table, capable of seating fourteen, stands elegantly upon the polished grey floor. A tea chest and urn from the original Dutch *walauwa* lie along the lower steps. Saskia designed the black dining lights, which hang from the overhead metal rafter.

overleaf
left Every detail of this child's bedroom is painted or clothed in snow white with the exception of a pared down wooden desk and three leather stools. The room is accessed by its own private staircase, situated in the studio. The double doors at the rear lead to a balcony that looks north across the courtyard to the jungles of Weligama.

overleaf
top right The bedroom in the attic has a haunting ambience, dominated by a large communion tapestry of Jesus preparing to drink from the holy chalice. A pair of wooden children's chairs highlights the dreamlike nature of the room.

overleaf
below right Like the child's bedroom, the bathroom is awash with white – enamel sinks, shelves, dustbins, towels and tiled floor. A red medical box stands out dramatically on the top shelf.

galapita

A turn off from the main Kataragama – Buttala road rumbles slowly down a dirt track bordered by rushes and paddy fields before terminating at what appears to be a cottage of thatch and clay. The cottage is in fact a single wall and the scruffy blue door at its heart forms the principal entrance to Galapita, one of the most exciting new additions to Sri Lanka's burgeoning eco-tourism industry.

The blue door leads into a promising fifty-two-acre wonderland of newly planted trees (palmyra, frangipani, kohomba, mango, banana and kumbuk), vegetables, herbs and medicinal plants. The horizon swirls deep over rice paddies into the distant mountains of Yala. Two miles to the north rises Galapita Gala (literally "a rock atop a rock"), a monumental boulder spread-eagled upon another boulder. To the south, the vast Pelawatte sugarcane plantations form an interminable patchwork bound by forest copses and jungle scrub. One is swiftly overcome by a peace of mind inevitable to anyone who has just left the frantic highways of Sri Lanka and come to rest in a jungle.

A short walk down a forest track leads to the rocky banks of the Manik Ganga, the fabled River of Gems. On this visit, the river's velocity was somewhat tempered by the unexpected delay of the south west monsoon, but during the latter days of the rainy season it becomes a raging torrent. A footbridge suspended some fifteen metres above connects the two riverbanks. Thepiyo, koori and fresh water prawns wallow in the river below.

The principal base of Galapita lies just across the footbridge on the southern banks of the river. It was here that Rukman de Fonseka first came when walking through the jungles on a pilgrimage to the sacred site of Katargama. De Fonseka, scion of a prominent Sri Lanka gem merchant family, had spent the previous night sleeping in a nearby Buddhist temple. He knew little of the Manik Ganga save for whispers of its propensity at concealing large gems. Following the riverbank he came across a beautifully warped granite channel, the river waters forming a natural hierarchy of waterfalls and natural plunge pools. De Fonseka, an urban dweller by nature, was overcome by a sense of belonging. He slept beneath the stars that night, with nothing but a mat and a hat. In 1996 he returned to Galapita and built the first hut. The following year he extended the hut and invited friends to stay. Since 2000, Galapita has been open to paying guests enabling de Fonseka to provide full time employment to seven local villagers, and a further fifteen on the farm.

above The principal entrance to Galapita is a scruffy blue door set into a simple clay wall and roofed with thatch, creating a restrained yet magical touch.

opposite The open air, dining pavilion stands at the eastern edge of the property. The table and benches are constructed from contoured planks of satinwood and the legs of gnarled kumbuk.

The eco-lodge presently consists of five detached bedrooms, a central living room, a dining pavilion, two bathrooms and a kitchen. Each building is carefully secured upon the smooth granite river banks. All bedrooms are open to the elements, encouraging guests to commune with the surrounding nature. The project, drawn out over eight years, involved a collaboration between local carpenter Ruperatne, interior designer Ajith Jayasundera and de Fonseka as supervisor. In keeping with the latters' stated priority of ecological sustainability, the structural design is deliberately primitive. Walls of clay and bamboo are surmounted by low eave roofs of illuk thatch, in turn supported by a simple yet effective sequence of treated weera and palm beams.

There is something intensely calming about living in splendid isolation on the side of a river such as the Manik Ganga, Sri Lanka's most venerable waterway. Twenty miles downstream, pilgrims of practically every denomination immerse themselves in these same sacred waters before entering Katargama, the greatest shrine in southern Sri Lanka. De Fonseka himself returns to Galapita whenever the opportunity arises. "Finding it was quite possibly the best thing that ever happened to me," he says.

above A fifteen-metre high suspension footbridge of kumbuk wood runs thirty-three metres across the Manik Ganga, connecting the organic garden to the principal base.
opposite above Snakegourd, drumstick, long beans, tomatoes, garlic and green chilies are prepared on the kitchen table.
opposite below Steps from the dining room on the eastside lead down towards the river. Illuk thatch on palm beams forms an effective and waterproof roof. The principle material employed in the walls and floor is clay.

overleaf
left In the principal living area, humble yet enchanting cotton-covered sofas of molded clay invite repose around tables of driftwood. Planters' chairs of wicker and teak offer alternative seats.

overleaf
right A satinwood tree house stands twelve metres above ground in the bough of a palu tree, offering spectacular views of surrounding paddy fields and jungle to the mountain of Galapita Gala beyond.

above The net-encased bed in the honeymooner's bedroom consists of a thin mattress of natural foam rubber resting on an antique bed from the Northern Province. A clay bench to the right is colourfully decorated with red and yellow cushions.

opposite The Manik Ganga rolls seawards through its granite corridor. To the right, the kumbuk pillars of the honeymooner's thatched cottage occupy a suitably discreet setting to the west of the property.

the river house

The River House stands on the southern banks of the Madhu Estuary. Here the great waters of the Madhu Ganga, make their final surge into the Indian Ocean. In the 18th century, such a fertile location proved invaluable to Dutch merchants who planted the estuarine landscape with cinnamon, a species native to Sri Lanka. By the 1960s, the country's cinnamon trade was in decline and the Madhu estates were abandoned.

In 2002, Colombo-based interior designer Nayantara Fonseka acquired a seven-acre site amid the once flourishing cinnamon belt. The property included a dilapidated wattle and daub bungalow from the 1950s. Between August 2003 and July 2004, she orchestrated the conversion of the bungalow into a spectacular riverside guest house. It was a laborious process, commencing with the reconstruction of the original termite and dry rot riddled walls. A new Romanesque villa was then constructed around these walls, consisting of a main living area and four separate suites. Each suite consists of a generously proportioned bedroom and spacious bathroom. The latter takes full advantage of Sri Lanka's prime weather patterns and allows for both indoor and outdoor bathing. Likewise, each suite has its own shaded courtyard enabling guests to enjoy the sounds of nature in private.

The River House stands on a raised hillock looking north to the river. When Fonseka began the reconstruction, the river was out of sight, submerged in a rampant wilderness that had taken over the former cinnamon estate. A dozen men from the nearby villages of Balapitiya and Ambalangoda were recruited to clear the unruly jungle. In gratitude, a large number of hitherto neglected fruit trees – olive, goraka, mango, coconut and lime – began to bear fruit again. The land was then replanted with vegetables, spices, rice and further fruits that now adorn the River House's acclaimed dinner menu. A swimming pool and pavilion were subsequently set into the garden, and a fifth completely detached honeymoon suite built a short distance from the riverbank. The latter additions are connected to the main house by a series of interweaving paths, each beholding an alternative view of the river marsh, paddy fields and rejuvenated garden.

In furnishing the property, Fonseka took a similar approach to that which she had successfully employed at "Taru Villas" in Bentota. She travelled around Sri Lanka from the northern Jaffna peninsula to Galle, selecting specific pieces of furniture from antique shops and traders along the way. Some of the "Jaffna" doors and windows originally belonged to houses in the north and east destroyed

above An abandoned cinnamon estate on the jungle-clad banks of the Madhu Ganga delta provides the basis for the "River House", one of the most impressive new additions to Sri Lanka's portfolio of boutique hotels. The Madhu Ganga, which rises in the Central Highlands, powers through the estate on its course to the sea at nearby Balapitiya.

in the civil war. She also ventured to Thailand and India where she sourced many of the various fabrics and decorative features. Where she could, Fonseka stylised the property with custom-built sofas, tables and box lamps.

The River House stands as a major testament to Fonseka's creative prowess and considerable energy. In the short time since it's official opening, the property has climbed to the uppermost ranks of Sri Lanka's most exceptional places to stay. The essence is peace – guided by the sound of the river and ocean, shaped by the beauty of the surrounding land.

above The River House adopts many traditional features of houses found in the Asian Tropics. Open-sided rooms, verandahs, courtyards and garden ponds allow free circulation of air and keep the rooms cool. The principal sitting room lies at ground level to the front of the house, looking down towards the Madhu Ganga. The sofas were designed by Fonseka and made by a local upholsterer. Chairs from South East Asia are grouped around an antique Dutch colonial table with "ball legs".

below A narrow void at the centre of the main building becomes a shaded retreat during the warmer hours. Designed by Fonseka, the sofas are framed by mirrors crafted from the panels of antique Jaffna doors.

right On the lower level terrace, antique fretwork combines with detachable *pettagama* legs to form a table surmounted by a tall vase of white frangipani blossoms. **opposite** The bedrooms are designed with a balanced precision that flows smoothly from a *dhurrie* (a North Indian handloom cotton rug) in the foreground to an opening in the back wall. The bed itself is made of polished grey cement extending to the left and right of the bedhead to form a useful sideboard against the rear wall. Taru designed the bedside lamps. At the foot of the bed a small Kandyan money-box rests upon an antique *pettagama*.

On the lower reaches of the hillside property, the sound of Madhu Ganga's rushing waters echoes off the jungle trees surrounding the swimming pool and pavilion.

FACT FILE

Official Name Democratic Socialist Republic of Sri Lanka (changed from Ceylon in 1972).
Population 19.2 million (2004).
Climate Tropical.
Area 66,000 sq km.
Highest Point Pidurutalagala (2524 m), Adam's Peak (2224 m).
Religion Sinhalese Buddhist (70%), Tamil Hindu (18%), Muslim (7.5%), Christian (4.5%).
Ethnic Groups Sinhalese (74%), Tamil (18%), Moor (7%), Burgher, Malay, Chinese and Vedda (1%).
Language Tamil, Sinhalese, English, Dutch, Wanniyala-aetto. Note: English is commonly used in government and is spoken competently by about 10% of the population.
Provinces Central, North Central, North Eastern, North Western, Sabaragamuwa, Southern Uva and Western.
Major Cities Colombo (capital), Kandy, Jaffna, Nuwara Eliya, Galle, Trincomalee, Batticaloa, Matara, Kurunegala, Anuradhapura, Polonnaruwa.
Legal System English Common Law mixed with Roman-Dutch, Muslim, Sinhalese, Tamil and customary law.
Economy Garments, tea, coconuts, fishing, tourism, gems.
Public Holidays Sri Lanka has more public holidays than any other country in the world. Many of the 26 public holidays are based on the lunar calendar, so dates vary from year to year depending on the Gregorian calendar. The full moon (*poya*) holidays are the most frequent but there are also festivals for Hindus, Christians and Muslims.
Principal Sports Cricket, football, tennis.

PLACES TO STAY

AMANGALLA
10 Church Street, Fort, Galle, Sri Lanka
Tel: +94 91 2233388
Fax: +94 91 2233355
Email: amangalla@amanresorts.com
Website: www.amanresorts.com

APA VILLA
78 M.S. Matara Road, Thalpe, Sri Lanka
Tel / Fax: +94 91 2283320
Mobile: +94 77 7317299
Email: harrison@sri.lanka.net
Website: www.villa-srilanka.com

THE BEACH HOUSE
Tangalle, Sri Lanka
Tel: +94 91 2232569
Fax: +94 91 2232568
Email: eden@villasinsrilanka.com
Website: www.villasinsrilanka.com

COLOMBO HOUSE
23 Gregory's Road, Colombo 7, Sri Lanka
Tel: +94 11 2688017
Fax: +94 11 2671817
Email: harrison@sri.lanka.net
Website: www.villa-srilanka.com

DOORNBERG
18 Upper Dickson Road, Galle, Sri Lanka
Tel: +94 91 4380275
Fax: +94 91 2222624
Email: sunhouse@sri.lanka.net
Website: www.thesunhouse.com

GALAPITA
Buttala Road, Uva Province, Sri Lanka
Tel: +94 11 2508755
Fax: +94 11 2508756
Email: paradiselanka@sltnet.lk
Website: www.galapita.com

HELGA'S FOLLY
Off Mahamaya Mawatha, Kandy, Sri Lanka
Tel: +94 81 4474314 or +94 81 2234571
Fax: +94 81 4479370
Website: www.helgasfolly.com

ILLUKETIA
Ellukkatiya Watta, Wanchawela, Galle, Sri Lanka
Tel: +94 91 4381411
Fax: +94 91 4381410
Email: harrison@sri.lanka.net
Website: www.villa-srilanka.com

KAHANDA KANDA
Koggala Lake, Galle, Sri Lanka
Tel: +94 91 2232569
Fax: +94 91 2232568
Email: eden@villasinsrilanka.com
Website: www.villasinsrilanka.com

THE LAST HOUSE
Pubudu Mawatha, Seenimodera, Nakalagamuwa, Sri Lanka
Tel: +94 81 4921394
Fax: +94 81 2420846
Email: info@thekandyhouse.com
Website: www.thelasthouse-mahawella.com

THE LIGHTHOUSE HOTEL
Dadella, Galle, Sri Lanka
Tel: +94 91 2224017 or +94 91 2223744
Fax: +94 91 2224021
Email: hotels@jetwing.lk
Website: www.lanka.net/jetwing/lighthouse

RAFTER'S RETREAT
The Rafter's Retreat, Hilland Group, Kitulgala, Sri Lanka
Tel: +94 36 2287598
Fax: +94 36 2287509
Email: channap@itmin.net or channape@sltnet.lk

THE RIVER HOUSE
70 Uththama Nyana Mawatha, Walagedera, Balapitiya, Sri Lanka
Tel: +94 11 4724363 or +94 77 7748064
Fax: +94 11 4724362
Email: theriverhouse@taruvillas.com
Website: www.taruvillas.com

TAPROBANE ISLAND
Taprobane Island, Weligama Bay, Sri Lanka
Tel: +94 91 4380275
Fax: +94 91 2222624
Email: sunhouse@sri.lanka.net
Website: www.taprobaneisland.com

TARU VILLAS
146/6 Galle Road, Robolgoda, Bentota, Sri Lanka
Tel: +94 11 4724363 or +94 77 7748064
Fax: +94 11 4724362
Email: taprobana@taruvillas.com
Website: www.taruvillas.com

ULPOTHA
Tel: +44 870 444 2702
Email: info@ulpotha.com
Website: www.ulpotha.com

VICTORIA
Matara Road, Thalpe, Galle, Sri Lanka
Tel: +94 91 2283523
Email: harrison@sri.lanka.net
Website: www.villa-srilanka.com

STOCKISTS

ART GALLERIES

Fnominal Space Gallery
Galle Face Court
Colombo 3

Gallery 71
71 Pedlar Street
Fort
Galle
Tel: +94 91 4385394
Email: announshka@wow.lk

Paradise Road Studio House
12 Alfred House Gardens
Colombo 3
Tel: +94 11 2506844
Fax: +94 11 2556564
Email: prgallery@eureka.lk

FASHION, STYLE, ANTIQUES & ACCESSORIES

Agasti Jewels
62 Havelock Road
Colombo 5
Tel: +94 11 2587137

Arena
338 Darley Road
Colombo 10
Tel: +94 11 555538

Barefoot Gallery & Bookshop
706 Galle Road
Colombo 3
Tel: +94 11 2580114
Fax. +94 11 2576936
Website: www.barefootceylon.com

Elephant Walk
61 Ward Road
Colombo 7
Tel: +94 11 269056

The Gallery Café
2 Alfred House Road
Colombo 3
Tel: +94 11 2582162

Hermitage
28 Gower Street
Colombo 5
Tel: +94 11 2502198

ARTS, ANTIQUES & COLLECTIBLES

House of Fashion
28 Duplication Road
Colombo 5

CLOTHING, TOYS, SPORTS GOODS, BABY ITEMS, BATH TOWELS & MATS

Jayakody Florists
Shirohana Atelier
21/3 Alfred House Gardens
Colombo 3
Tel: +94 11 2598277
Fax: +94 11 2447760
Email: huejay@slt.lk

Mimimango
40A Leyn Baan Street
Fort
Galle
Tel: +94 77 7513473

The Oasis Company
18 Station Road
Bambalapitiya
Colombo 4

Odel Unlimited
5 Alexander Place
Colombo 7
Tel: +94 11 2682712
Email: info@eodel.lk
Website: www.eodel.lk
(Hugely popular clothes and accessories shop. Outlets at Majestic City, Colombo 4, Trans Asia Hotel, Colombo 2 and Odel Warehouse, 38, Dickmans Road, Colombo 5.)

Paradise Road
213 Dharmapala Mawatha
Colombo 7
Tel: +94 11 2686043 or +94 11 2689874
Fax: +94 11 2689874
Email: paradiserd@eureka.lk

Paradise Road – The Gallery Shop
2 Alfred House Road
Off Alfred House Gardens
Colombo 3
Tel: +94 11 2582162 or +94 11 2556563
Fax: +94 11 2556564
Email: prgallery@eureka.lk

Raux Brothers
7 De Fonseka Road
Colombo 5
Tel: +94 11 5339016
Email: kraux@eureka.lk
Website: www.asiabusiness.com/sl/rauxbrothers

Samadhi Centre – Antiques & Meditation
761 Peradeniya Road
Kandy
Mobile: +94 77 7710013
Tel: +94 81 4470925
Fax: +94 81 5740600
Email: waruna@eureka.lk
Website: www.samadhicentre.com

Serendib Gallery
36 Rosmead Place
Cinnamon Gardens
Colombo 7
Tel: +94 11 4710002
Email: info@theserendibgallerycom
Website: www.theserendibgallery.com
(Rare Sri Lankan maps, porcelain, furniture etc.)

Southern Antiques & Reproductions
32 Urawatta
Galle Road
Ambalangoda
Tel: +94 91 2258005

PROPERTY – RENT & BUY

Lanka Real Estate
Tel: +94 77 7235775
Email: info@lankarealestate.com
Website: www.lankarealestate.com
Contact: Ivan Robinson

Eden Villas
65A Lighthouse St.
Fort
Galle
Tel: +94 91 2232569
Email: eden@villasinsrilanka.com
Website: www.villasinsrilanka.com

Charles G. Hulse
16 Parawa Street
Fort
Galle
Tel / Fax: +94 91 2234161
Email: hulsecg@eureka.lk
Website: www.charleshulse.com

BOOKSHOPS

Barefoot Books
706 Galle Road
Colombo 3
Tel: +94 11 2589305
Email: sales@barefoot.lk

Odel
5 Alexandra Place
Lipton Circus
Colombo 7
Tel: +94 11 2682712 or
+94 11 4722200
Email: mail@eodel.com

Vijitha Yapa
Unity Plaza
Colombo 3
Tel: +94 11 2596960
Email: vijiyapa@sri.lanka.net

Lakehouse
100 Sir Chittampalam A. Gardiner Mawatha
Colombo 2
Tel: +94 11 4734137
Fax: +94 11 2430582

FURTHER READING

Agrawal, O. P., and Wickramasinghe, N. A., *Materials and Techniques of Ancient Wall Paintings of Sri Lanka*, New Delhi, 2002

Ahir, D. C., *Glimpses of Sri Lankan Buddhism*, New Delhi, 2000

Baker, M., *The Swimming Pool – Inspiration and Style from Around the World*, Thames & Hudson, London, 2005

Baldaeus, P., *A Description of the Great and Most Famous Isle of Ceylon*, New Delhi, 1996 (reprint)

Bassett, R. H., *Romantic Ceylon: Its History, Legend and Story*, New Delhi, 1997 (reprint)

Berriedale, K. A., *Buddhist Philosophy in India and Ceylon*, New Delhi, 1995 (reprint)

Brito, C., *The Yalpana-Vaipava-Malai or The History of the Kingdom of Jaffna*, New Delhi, 1999 (reprint)

Burns, N., *Safari Style*, Thames & Hudson, London, 1998

Burrows, S. M., *The Buried Cities of Ceylon: A Guide Book to Anuradhapura and Polonaruwa*, New Delhi, 1999 (reprint)

Campbell, J., *Excursions Adventures and Field-Sports in Ceylon*, New Delhi, 1999 (reprint)

Carpenter, E., *From Adam's Peak to Elephanta: Sketches in Ceylon and India*, London, 1999 (reprint)

Cave, H. W., *Golden Tips: A Description of Ceylon and Its Great Tea Industry*, New Delhi, 1994 (reprint)

Cave, H. W., *The Ruined Cities of Ceylon*, New Delhi, 1999 (reprint)

Chopra, P. N., and Chopra, P., *Monuments of the Raj: British Buildings in India, Pakistan, Bangladesh, Sri Lanka and Myanmar*, New Delhi, 1999

Cliff, S., and de Chabaneix, G., *The Way We Live: Alfresco*, Thames & Hudson, London, 2005

Cliff, S., and de Chabaneix, G., *The Way We Live: Making Homes/Creating Lifestyles*, Thames & Hudson, London, 2003

Coomaraswamy, A. K., *Mediaeval Sinhalese Art: Being a Monograph on Mediaeval Sinhalese Arts and Crafts, Mainly as Surviving in the Eighteenth Century, with an Account of the Structure of Society and the Status of the Craftsmen*, New Delhi, 2003 (reprint)

De Silva, C. R., *Ceylon Under the British Occupation, 1795–1833*, New Delhi, 1995 (reprint)

Devendra, T., *Sri Lanka: The Emerald Island*, New Delhi, 1996

Freeman, M., *In the Oriental Style – A Sourcebook of Decoration and Design*, Thames & Hudson, London, 1990

Freeman, M., *The Spirit of Asia – Journeys to the Sacred Places of the East*, Thames & Hudson, London, 2000

Gerson Da Cunha, J., *Memoir on the History of the Tooth-Relic of Ceylon with a Preliminary Essay on the Life and System of Gautama Buddha*, New Delhi, 1996

Gunasekara, B., *The Rajavaliya or A Historical Narrative of Sinhalese Kings from Vijaya to Vimala Dharma Surya II*, New Delhi, 1995 (reprint)

Harischandra, B. W., *The Sacred City of Anuradhapura*, New Delhi, 1998 (reprint)

Harrison, J., *A Field Guide to the Birds of Sri Lanka*, Oxford, 1999

Helmi, R., and Walker, B., *Bali Style*, Thames & Hudson, London, 1995

Jeyaratnam Wilson, A., *Sri Lankan Tamil Nationalism: Its Origins and Development in the Nineteenth and Twentieth Centuries*, New Delhi, 2001 (reprint)

Jones-Bateman, R., *An Illustrated Guide to the Buried Cities of Ceylon*, New Delhi, 1994 (reprint)

Khanna, S. K., and Sudarshan, K. N., *Encyclopaedia of South Asia: Sri Lanka*, New Delhi, 1998

Knighton, W., *Forest Life in Ceylon*, London, 1998 (reprint)

Knox, R., *An Historical Relation of the Island of Ceylon in the East Indies*, New Delhi, 2004 (reprint)

Lee, G., *Spa Style Asia – Therapies, Cuisines, Spas*, Thames & Hudson, London, 2003

Lloyd, B., *The Colours of Southern India*, Thames & Hudson, London, 1999

Malhotra, I., *Dynasties of India and Beyond: Pakistan, Sri Lanka, Bangladesh*, New Delhi, 2003

Menasche, E. L., *Ceylon: Island of Gems*, New Delhi, 2004 (reprint)

Munro, I. S. R., *The Marine and Fresh Water Fishes of Ceylon*, New Delhi, 2000

Musaeus Higgins, M., *Poya Days*, New Delhi, 1999 (reprint)

Musaeus Higgins, M., *The Ramayana: A Historical Play of Jambudwipa and Lanka*, New Delhi, 2000 (reprint)

Musaeus-Higgins, M., *Stories from the History of Ceylon for Children*, New Delhi, 2000 (reprint)

Narayan Swamy, M. R., *Inside an Elusive Mind: Prabhakaran: The First Profile of the World's Most Ruthless Guerrilla Leader*, New Delhi, 2003

Nissanka, H. S. S. (ed.), *Maha Bodhi Tree in Anuradhapura, Sri Lanka: The Oldest Historical Tree in the World*, New Delhi, 1996 (reprint)

Ondaatje, M., *Anil's Ghost*, London, 2000

Ondaatje, M., *Running in the Family*, London, 1983

Parker, H., *Village Folk-Tales of Ceylon*, New Delhi, 2003

Phear, J. B., *The Aryan Village in India and Ceylon*, New Delhi, 1995 (reprint)

Pieris, P. E., *Ceylon and the Hollanders: 1658–1796*, New Delhi, 1999 (reprint)

Pole, J., *Ceylon Stone Implements*, New Delhi, 2000

Purnalingam Pillai, M. S., *Ravana: The Great King of Lanka*, New Delhi, 2003 (reprint)

Rettie, C., *Things Seen in Ceylon: The Description of a Beautiful Island and the Novel and Interesting Town and Country Life of Its People*, New Delhi, 2002 (reprint)

Richardson, P., *Contemporary Natural*, Thames & Hudson, London, 2002

Senaveratne, J. M., *The Date of Buddha's Death and Ceylon Chronology*, New Delhi, 2000

Senaveratne, J. M., *Royalty in Ancient Ceylon: During the Period of the "Great Dynasty"*, New Delhi, 2000 (reprint)

Senaveratne, J. M., *The Story of the Sinhalese: From the Most Ancient Times up to the End of "The Mahavansa" or Great Dynasty*, New Delhi, 1997 (reprint)

Singh Bhasin, A., *India in Sri Lanka: Between Lion and the Tigers*, New Delhi, 2004

Skeen, W., *Adam's Peak: Legendary Traditional and Historic Notes of the Samanala and Sri-Pada*, New Delhi, 1997 (reprint)

Slesin, S., *Indian Style*, Thames & Hudson, London, 1990

Smither J. G., *Architectural Remains: Anuradhapura, Ceylon*, New Delhi, 1994 (reprint)

Still, J., *Index to the Mahawansa: Together with Chronological Table of Wars and Genealogical Trees*, New Delhi, 1999 (reprint)

Storey, H., *A Ceylon Sportsman's Diary: An Account of the Author's Shooting Experiences from 1909 to 1920 Inclusive*, New Delhi, 2000 (reprint)

Street-Porter, T., *Tropical Houses: Living in Natural Paradise*, Thames & Hudson, London, 2000

Tanaka, M., *Patrons, Devotees and Goddesses: Ritual and Power among the Tamil Fishermen of Sri Lanka*, New Delhi, 1997 (reprint)

Walters, A., *Palms and Pearls or Scenes in Ceylon*, New Delhi, 1997 (reprint)

Wickramasinghe, N., *Civil Society in Sri Lanka: New Circles of Power*, New Delhi, 2001

Williams, H., *Ceylon: Pearl of the East*, New Delhi, 2002

Wright, A. (ed.), *Twentieth Century Impressions of Ceylon: Its History, People, Commerce, Industries and Resources*, London, 1907

Ypma, H., *Hip Hotels: Orient*, Thames & Hudson, London, 2005

ACKNOWLEDGMENTS

This book would not have been possible without the kindness and patience of many people. As such, our sincere thanks to Ranjan and Shaunagh Aluwihare, Alex Barrett, Helga de Silva Perera Blow, George Cooper, Sherry Crowley, Priscynthica Dissanayake, Geoffrey Dobbs, Rob Drummond, Jack and Jo Eden, Bruce Fell-Smith, Harriet Fennell, Shanth Fernando, Rukman Fonseka, Sanjiva Gautamadasa, Nikki and Bob Harrison, Eduard and Announshka Hempel, Hans Hoefer, Charlie Hulse, Tim Jacobson, Hugo Jellet, Hugh Karunanayak, Ann Kennedy, Ally Moore, Nicola Morris, Samy and Reshan Pavel, Channa Perera, Jaya and Alex Pieris, Pierre and Saskia Pringiers, Olivia Richli, Henri Tatham, Dr Aelred Samarakoon, Giles Scott, Joe Simpson, Taru and Leana, and Chandra Wickramasinghe.

Thanks also to the Sri Lanka Tourist Board (www.srilankatourism.org), the Lighthouse Hotel and Partnership Travel.